Right Side Out

In-tune Within, To Be In Harmony With The World

Annah Moore

Right Side Out
In-tune Within, To Be In Harmony With The World

Cover painting by Bob Thompson, copyright © 1964.
Used with permission.

To all who have the courage to be themselves.
And to those who stand beside them.

TABLE OF CONTENTS

Foreword

The phrase "right side out" can bring to mind many different images and memories, perhaps the most common being that of clothing that is right side out. But to me, the phrase "right side out" has much deeper meaning. It is about being who you are—it's about the outside reflecting who you are inside, about having your true right side out. Being right side out is not something most people have a problem with; they just are who they are, and their outside reflects who they are inside. But some people, like me, often struggle for years, sometimes decades, with a perplexing situation: we fight a war against ourselves to keep our right side in, where no one else can see it. The reasons for this are deep and complex, but once we understand who we are and that the forces keeping us from being true to ourselves come from within us, we stand a strong chance of finally being right side out.

I also think of right side out as a reference to the right side of the brain, the creative side, being allowed to extend itself outward, from the person to the world, through art. Art is one the greatest tools for communication we have. We can release the pressures within us through art. We can show our love and hatred through art. We can inspire people with art, and we can embarrass people with it as well. Perhaps most importantly, art can be an incredibly powerful tool for healing and recovery.

Another meaning of "right side out" involves making the right choices in your life—choosing to do the right thing and following through with it. In order to make the right choices in any given moment, we must be free from guilt for not living up to others' expectations. We must be free from shame about who we really are. And we must be unafraid to do whatever it takes to fight for our very existence, and to find peace and harmony in our lives. Only when we are true to ourselves, in tune with who we are, can we be in tune with the symphony of life.

"It's what's *inside* that matters anyway…" a friend of mine said to me one sunny day.

"That's exactly right," I replied. "And because the inside matters so much, you should understand why the outside must reflect who I am inside." She just raised an eyebrow and looked away.

x

Part I:
The Core of the Matter

The Conundrum

There is no easy way to explain to people about myself and the life I have lived. Most of the time, when I tell people stories from my life, they generally seem to zone out. Perhaps my voice is so soothing that they fall asleep! Or maybe they don't believe me, or it could just be too much to comprehend. Maybe they are lost in befuddlement. I don't know. They probably just think I'm full of it. Little do they know! If they could only see what I have seen! When I was little, you would never have known that I had such a big problem that affected everything I did, everything I thought about, and every waking moment of my life. You might have looked at me playing with my friends and thought, "Oh, that's such a happy kid." But you could not have seen the inner turmoil I was going through.

Even I had a hard time seeing it for what it was.

From my earliest memories, I knew something was funky. When I was about six years old, I would be lying in bed, thinking about myself as I drifted off to sleep, and I would know something was not quite right. It wasn't that who I was as a person wasn't right, it was that who I was inside wasn't consistent with what I was on the outside. At that time, however, it was not possible for me to pinpoint the incongruity. I lived my life much like any other child; I had loving parents, played games with my friends, rode my bicycle up and down the block, and played street hockey in the street or baseball in the empty lot. I must have seemed normal to others, but there was always something strange going on behind the scenes that no one else ever saw. To this day, if I had never said or done anything about it, and if I had been able to hide it, no one would have ever known that

something was different about me. It was there from the very first memories I have of my life.

Because the years before puberty and sexuality are rather androgynous, and even though my body sex and my gender identity didn't match, at that time they didn't feel as incongruent as they would in the years to come. At that young age, I didn't have much of a grasp of what it meant to be male or female, aside from the usual penis equals boy/vagina equals girl association. Even that concept, however, was askew for me because of my transsexual condition. I never quite grasped what it meant to be a boy or a girl. I did not fully realize it at the time, but I was both a boy and a girl! I wonder if those who do not suffer from this condition can even imagine what it is like to be one inside the other, a female self inside a male body. The phrase "a woman trapped in a man's body" rings true, and if current medical theory and research hold true, it is very much a reality. The International Journal of Transgenderism online contains a wealth of research information. One article of particular interest is called *A Sex Difference in the Human Brain and its Relation to Transsexuality*. Those of us with the transsexual condition are most easily described as simply being inside the wrong body. In this world of binary sexuality, most people do not even realize that there is more to human life than male and female. There are variations of every kind in between. The problem is not that transsexuals are different, or that we do not fit into the binary sexual system; the problem is the system itself and the misconception or, perhaps more accurately, the misleading idea that anyone who is not a member of one or the other sexes is abnormal. That is a fallacy and absolutely untrue. I, and countless others like me, are living proof of that.

The problem is also exacerbated by the fact that many in the social and medical arenas do not acknowledge that this is a condition that is treatable, like any other treatable medical condition. We are born with the condition, but after we move beyond it, through counseling, hormone therapy, and perhaps surgery, we overcome it. Then we are no longer transsexuals; rather we become the woman, or man, we should have been in the first place.

The Girl No One Knew

My earliest memories are from when my family—Mom, Dad, and I—lived in Philadelphia, from when I was three until I was two weeks shy of my eighth birthday. We lived on a block of row houses that were close to where Dad was teaching; he was a professor at Drexel University. I clearly remember the street and the friends I had there, many neat kids of every nationality and ethnic background. I didn't think twice about where I was growing up at the time, although now I am grateful that I got to live in that environment. I believe that it has helped give me an unbiased view of others, and I have always felt that race and color just don't matter. It's the person who matters. Philly was where I learned to ride a bike, where I learned how to skate, and where I learned how not to do a one-handed jump off a curb on my bike!

I had only a small number of friends there, which is consistent with how things have been in all of the places that I've lived. For me, friendship is all about quality, not quantity: I would rather have a few very close friends, with whom I can share openness and honesty, than a bunch of people I don't know very well. Even with my handfuls of friends, I was something of a loner, mostly because I did not feel as though I fit in very well. I would end up being with the boys because that was where I thought I was expected to be and also because they seemed to want to hang out with me, although there were many girls I enjoyed playing with. The girls' activities always interested me, but at the same time, I did enjoy playing in the dirt with cars and playing cowboys-and-Indians and cops-and-robbers. Sometimes I think that if I had been female from the very beginning, I still would have enjoyed those kinds of things. Perhaps I would have been somewhat tomboyish, but it is hard to say. Those early years were not too bad because for the most part I felt somewhat normal. Yet it was at that time that my inner confusion would expose itself on a conscious level, and I would wonder why I wanted to be with the girls instead of the boys. Moments like those were when I started to realize that something about me was off; I just didn't have the experience and understanding to figure out what it was.

Looking back on those experiences and wondering why I enjoyed "boy play," like GI Joes, cars, cops-and-robbers, and all the rest, I suspect that a lot of the "why" had to do with hormonal balance. Now that I've been on estrogen for a few years, I am very aware that a person's perspective and attitude definitely shift depending on which hormone is dominant. However, in my very early years, I think that I felt pressure from my peers and social groups to conform and fit in, as most of us do. I think that this is why I often "went with the crowd"—"the crowd" being the boys.

It is interesting, the things we remember once we start to think about bits and pieces of the past. One memory leads to another, and all of a sudden we are remembering things that totally take us aback. It is amazing how much information we have stored in our brains, and how much of it tends to get blocked out or "forgotten." It's still there, though; you just have to want to see it.

One of the things that I must have blocked out for many years was the nickname Mom gave me when I was younger: "Mister Perfect." She didn't mean it in a demeaning or insulting way; she really meant it. It was so ironic, though, because I was obviously not perfect, and I surely was no "mister"! It created quite a name to try to live up to, though, and I did try, for so many years, to be Mister Perfect; I couldn't let Mom down, so I did everything I could to maintain a semblance of what that name suggested. She did not know that I was going through all the inner turmoil that I was; she really thought I was perfect. And in a sense, I guess I was as close to it as one could appear, because I learned how to make myself appear flawless to others, mainly to protect myself from being emotionally hurt, but more so to protect them from emotional hurt or stress.

These are the kinds of things we people pleasers do; we do almost anything and everything we can in order to please the ones we care about and to keep from hurting them emotionally, even if it means sacrificing our own happiness, our own emotional well-being, or our own selves. During my formative years, when I should have been forming into "Miss Perfect," I was forming into someone who hid her flaws and confusion and emotional turmoil exceedingly well. I believe that this explains why my emotional relationship with my parents suffered so deeply throughout the years, and why I became so distant from them, and subsequently them from me, for so long. It became almost impossible not to be deeply affected by this emotional separation because the people who I should have been able to turn to first were the people I was most afraid to tell. I can only imagine how this scenario plays out for other children, other families, who go through similar situations, including those that do not involve transsexualism.

All this leads to so many emotional issues, the main one being repression. We end up stuffing emotions deep down inside in an effort to avoid them, but the problem with that comes when that which we are trying to avoid is *within* us, inherent to our being, and something we cannot avoid. There is no way to escape; we may try, with drugs or other methods, but eventually all that pent-up emotional energy will burst forth. Then is when we face the greatest trouble. For me, it wasn't until my teens that the pressure started coming close to popping my emotional repression balloon.

If They Could Only See What I See

When I was eight, we moved from Philadelphia to a small town in northern Arizona. What a change! We went from living in a row house in a massive city to a two-story house on an acre of forested land. I started third grade in our new town, and as things went, I was not a very good student. I sat staring out the window most of the time, as the hours passed by. I can clearly remember what I thought back then, often wondering if I were really a girl and if God or fate had played some wicked trick on me. I even thought, for quite some time, that all girls must have penises; after all, I was a girl, and I had one. Great confusion was an everyday part of life, although I tried hard to keep anyone else from knowing. I was afraid to soil my "perfect" image! I did not want to let anyone down, family and friends especially.

I would stare out the window of the classroom and watch the trees and clouds move in the wind, as I thought about things—like why I was feeling so "off" and not right somehow. It seemed that what my teacher was trying to teach just did not matter to me at all. There was something in me that was far more important, something calling out from inside me. I didn't know what it was exactly, but I remember wishing I were free, but free of what? I did not know.

Because of my trouble in school I was moved out of standard elementary school and into a private school, which Mom and Dad hoped would help me do better. It was a good move for me, because the environment was more open and I was able to express myself better in artistic forms, which I think were not emphasized enough in the standard elementary school. And as it turned out, I thrived on art and music, and they have been two of the primary driving forces in my life. I honestly think that if it were not for the arts,

I would not be here to write this book.

During that year in private school, I had my first kiss. I still remember the moment as if it were yesterday, and the awkwardness I felt then and the evening and days following. We were not officially boyfriend and girlfriend, but it was the first time for both of us. We didn't know what to do, especially me, and that made me even more confused when that was mixed with the growing internal confusion about myself I already had. One day, we were sharing an apple, and it just sort of happened. It was strange for us both, and we didn't do it again after that, but being with her was a distraction from my growing confusion; because it helped give me a false sense of fitting in, I didn't think much about my problem for a while. I figured, since I was a "boy" on the outside, that I was doing the right thing; doing what the world expected me to do. But even though it was the "right" thing to do, I just couldn't keep it going. I found myself not wanting to be involved with anyone because I didn't know where I fit in the grand scheme of boys and girls. Lessons about the expected relationships between boys and girls were imparted to me by my parents and all the other usual sources. So it was, in part, with this kiss that I figured out what my particular role in life was supposed to be, even though it profoundly went against what I felt inside. This lesson stuck, and stuck hard, and was a powerful force in my relationships to come.

As I moved out of private school and reentered public elementary school, I went back into the fourth grade. I had a wonderful teacher, Mrs. Stallings, who later died of breast cancer. She was beautiful, kind, and compassionate, smart and one of my all-time favorite teachers. I remember how much I wanted to be like her when I grew up, which was another confusing realization. Not only did I want to be kind and helpful the way she was, but also I wanted to be as pretty as she was. The confusion in me stepped up a notch that year, but that did not hold a candle to how intense it would eventually become.

Fifth grade, at the same elementary school, proved to be a turning point for me with regard to gender and sexuality. I began to notice the changes my fellow female classmates were going through, primarily the changes in their bodies: breasts were growing and butts were getting rounder and wider. They were paying more attention to their hair, and some even wore trace amounts of makeup. A strange question popped into my mind one day: "How come I'm not changing like that?"

The thought perplexed me. There it was. It was conscious now. It had risen from the depths of my being, from an unconscious confusion to a conscious question. I had a conversation with myself, probably in class as I stared out the window:

"Why don't I have boobs?"

"I don't know! Why would you want them?"

"I'm not sure…I just do. It seems normal."

"That's strange."

"Yeah. It's not like I want them as much as it seems like I'm supposed to have them, but I know I'm a boy on the outside and boys aren't supposed to have boobs."

"Exactly."

"But for some reason I still think that's how I'm supposed to be."

"Oh my God!"

This conscious realization of what had been going on in me for so many years already was too much to comprehend, and it was also embarrassing, even though I told no one. At that moment, major repression started. I suppose this was the first stage of the five phases of grief: denial. I convinced myself that this wasn't real and that I would forget about it as soon as the sun rose again the next day. The only problem waas that when the sun did rise, and I awoke, it was the first thing on my mind, and I woke up with it every single morning after that.

School grew into a frustrating situation for me, and it became a very complex balance of social life and internal self-management. I had to spend a lot of my mental energy trying to abate the rising thoughts in my mind about who, or what, I was. This led more and more to the "daydreaming" behavior I had shown in my earlier years. Trying to keep such thoughts at bay so that I could focus on school work became an almost impossible effort. Thinking back on it, it is easy to see the things I  needed to take care of before I could really move forward with my life. The only problem was that there was no way on earth that I could take care of the problem on my own, and there was no one else to whom I could turn, or so I thought. It's not that I had no one; even though I had withdrawn from them emotionally, Mom and Dad have always been there for me. In fact, they recently told me that they would have done whatever it took to help me find happiness if I had talked about it to them. But I was so confused, scared, embarrassed, and ashamed that I just couldn't talk to anyone about it. And again, repression became the mental tool I used to "fix" the problem.

At that time, I think the impact of social expectations really began to affect my ability to understand myself in gender and sexual terms, and because of such confusion, it seemed the best way to cope was to repress my growing feelings of incongruence. Besides, it was risky being a feminine boy, even though that is what I was, and I feared being labeled something I was not, like "queer" or "fag." By the time I was a teenager, I was sure I was not gay, but something was definitely wrong for me.

My bedroom was dark, save for the glow of the light coming through the window from the full moon outside, which cast its eerie glow on my wall and the drawings there, and on my ninth-grade school books and the junk on my little desk. I lay there on my side, pondering, feeling my usual feelings of "offness" and growing confusion about myself. I rolled onto my back and stared at the ceiling, barely visible above me. I was on my loft bed, the one Dad and Mom had built into my room. It was pretty cool, with a closet and a study area underneath. It made for some awesome fort building and was great fun for hiding in. Eventually, I had my first computer underneath the bed, on a little desk area. I remember Mom trying to teach me cursive writing in there. I never could write very well in cursive.

I stared at the ceiling in the dim lunar light. I reached down and touched myself, wondering why things were as they were and why they were not as I thought they should be. After more than a decade of life filled with subtle confusion and incongruence, like an ever-growing veil of numbness shrouding my mind, I was beginning to realize that the problem was either inside my head, or the problem was my body itself. Things did not feel right; "the parts" just did not fit. As they teach you in kindergarten, a square peg can't fit in a round hole; I realized in that moment that I, indeed, was that square peg that didn't fit, and it scared the hell out of me!

My stomach knotted. I rolled around, unable to sleep, unable to understand what was going on. I thought about the girls I knew at school. They were developing right, so why wasn't I? What was wrong with me? Maybe it wasn't just me, maybe it was that all girls start off as boys and become girls during puberty. But then, that did not make sense because girls were girls when they were born. Maybe all boys feel this way then! Yeah, that must be it; I am not alone! All boys feel this way, too! But that thought didn't last very long. I didn't have to ask anyone else, I just ended up realizing that boys are boys and girls are girls, and I was neither one; I was a girl in my head and a boy on the outside, and I was in a living hell! What could I do!? I couldn't tell anyone. I was too afraid. Afraid of being punished, afraid of being called a freak, or worse, whatever that might be— afraid of being sent away to a mental institution! Or an insane asylum! Well, there was only one thing I could do then— hide it. Keep it a secret. Never, ever, let anyone, anywhere, know about it.

Even as I thought about how much I wanted, and needed, to

be female, the seemingly irrational thoughts forced me to deal with them in ways that were not the most mentally healthy: repression, suppression, depression, and probably many more "essions"! How is a young adult supposed to deal with these kinds of issues? The vast majority of us cannot confide such thoughts to our parents at that age. Moreover, the last thing teenagers want to do is talk to their parents about sex, gender, or any other such things.

Around and around these circling trains of thought would go, finding nowhere to stop, no station of understanding to park in. My mind would basically go into a "deer in the headlights" mode, and I wouldn't be able to think about much of anything at all for a while, until I repressed the thoughts and moved on. That is how I spent a lot of my time in school.

I can't even remember how it started, but for whatever reasons, I was drawn to borrowing Mom's clothes in order to make myself feel better. Initially, I had no earthly idea why I was doing that; all I knew was that "being a girl" made me feel much more normal than being a boy. Simply changing my outward appearance helped dramatically because, if only temporarily, it brought my gender identity and my apparent body sex into congruity. Of course, I didn't understand it like that at the time.

There seemed to be a strange cycle of energy that waxed and waned between my desire to please my family and my fears and feelings of isolation. When I was in junior high school, the cycle seemed to be at its worst stage because I did not fully understand what was going on and because male hormones had started to increase in my body. My grandfather was a big Dallas Cowboys football fan, as were many of the men in my family, and football was almost always on the television when we would visit during the holidays. I recall many times sitting there watching football with my grandfather, and it was sometimes quite fun. Perhaps it was the ritual of it that was most fun, but I did enjoy watching the games a lot.

From my earliest recollection, my grandfather really wanted me to play football, especially in my pre-teen and teen years. In trying to allay my growing incongruence, in an attempt to hide myself for fear of being called more names, or worse, and in an attempt to please not only my grandfather but all my family, I had begun playing Pop Warner football when I was nine or ten years old.

I found it to be a pretty good way to release pent-up frustration and anger. I could put all that negative energy into pushing, shoving, smashing, and tackling the boys on the field! It was a great release! And it helped make me look more like Mister Perfect in the eyes of my family. I recall my grandfather asking me if I were ever going to be the quarterback or a running back or receiver. I told him I didn't think so since I played on the line, but what I really wanted was to play defense. He wasn't very happy with that. Perhaps he had set his expectations for me too high; I don't know.

Living up to being Mister Perfect became a tougher and eventually impossible task. I found that it was easier to exile myself to my room to draw, or to play outside by myself. That led to my perfecting of the art of acting, as well as to my becoming very good at detaching myself from my own reality. I would do anything and everything I could possibly think of to keep me distracted from my problem.

One of the things we do as male-to-female transsexuals (MtFs) during the course of our journey is try to prove primarily to ourselves, but also to those around us, that we are the boys or men our bodies allege we are. In doing so, we play the toughest games, including football and hockey, and we take on the manliest jobs, such as in the military or in construction, all in an attempt to either prove we are men or to try to make the problem go away.

It never works.

As a young person dealing with the transsexual condition, one of the toughest places to deal with was the boys' locker room, either during physical education class or when playing sports. During junior high school, being in a locker room full of boys, who were sometimes wearing nothing at all, and who were often snapping each other's' butts (or fronts, as was done to me more than once) with their towels, was an extremely nerve-wracking experience. I felt so self-conscious about my body already, without being in such a male environment. Having to disrobe and shower in front of twenty boys was not just embarrassing; it was, in many senses, humiliating. None of those boys ever knew how I felt, of course, and neither did my family; in fact, I was the only one who knew. And because of that, I felt that much more isolated and alone, and the feelings of shame and guilt compounded.

In ninth grade, I noticed a patch of hair starting to grow in the middle of my chest. I was devastated. I hated it. I figured it would just go away, but it spread like a virus! Then, as if that were not enough, a confusing attraction to girls began to take over my thoughts. The more testosterone that flowed through my veins, the more intense it all became. My body would respond as one might expect any boy's body to respond when seeing an attractive girl: the organ would swell in response. But as it did, and as I thought about how attractive certain girls were to me, I had other thoughts in my head, thoughts about how I wished I looked the way she did or that I would be like her someday. Sexual arousal became the pinnacle of confusion, because of this simultaneous excitement about women— for two different reasons.

I continued to borrow from Mom's closet for release from the tension. When Mom and Dad would leave the house to go out, I would raid her closet or drawers for things that fit me, things that would make me feel normal. Even if I were alone in my "normality," I felt better. I began playing with makeup and curling my hair with her curling iron. These were things I found to be a lot of fun; they were things I had wanted to do for a long time, and they helped me feel more like me. I can understand how some people would think that a boy doing these things would seem rather strange, but it is important to remember that I was not a boy!

Despite these moments of fun, the confusion in me grew. It began to take on a whole new characteristic: deep incongruence. The more I released the pressure inside my head, the more confused I became. The two aspects of who I was became separated, and my life became a duality. On one hand, I was the boy everyone knew, and on the other, I was the girl no one knew. I thought maybe I was gay and didn't want to admit it, but that didn't seem right. At the time, I wasn't exactly attracted to boys, and I also figured that being gay did not mean you wanted to be a girl; rather, you were a boy who liked other boys. I never was excited about "being a boy with a boy," so I knew I wasn't gay. Knowing that, and the fact that calling someone else a "fag" was popular in school, I tried everything I could to avoid being mislabeled. I tried not to be too outwardly feminine and tried to keep up appearances to save face, even though I was realizing what I really wanted in life was to just be myself—a girl.

During my junior high years, I became interested in computers. Mom and Dad sent me to a summer computer camp on Mingus Mountain. We stayed in log cabins, learned about computers and programming, and went on lots of nature hikes. I came home with a new passion, and not long thereafter, Mom and Dad bought me a Radio Shack TRS-80. Computers became a fantastic way to escape, both from the outside world and from myself. I especially got excited about video games and began writing my own simple video games using the Basic language. I progressed from that computer to a Commodore 64, which had a whopping sixteen colors and more memory. I began writing some pretty good code on that one. By the time I got to high school, I was already so good at programming that I was the teacher's assistant in the computer class. I was so good, in fact, that my fellow classmates often went to me for answers before they went to my teacher. I enjoyed sharing my knowledge with my classmates, and they seemed to enjoy what I shared. I made it fun for them, showing them the tricks I had learned for making cool things happen on the computer monitor.

Unfortunately, my grades were growing worse, even though I was so good at computers and programming. School continued to disinterest me, other than the social aspects of it, and my ever-growing incongruence was having a major effect on my life. I played the role I figured I was supposed to play, and I didn't create any waves in terms of breaking the gender rules, not that I really knew what they were.

One day, in my early teens, I was looking through a "men's magazine" when the full scope of my problem hit me. Up until then, I had been doing a good job of repressing the fact that I thought I should be female, so for the most part I did not consciously realize that's what I was feeling. The repression and feelings had been subtle until then, but the more I repressed, the more the feelings built up. The magazine experience was like popping the cap off a shaken bottle of soda— the realization burst forth along with a new awareness that hit me like a ton of bricks. As I flipped from page to page, I was amazed at the beauty of the women in the pictures. As I turned a page, at one point I said quietly to myself, "Wow, I wish I were her." I was floored.

I didn't know what to think.

I thought I was totally nuts!

I wished I were her? What the hell was I thinking? I tossed the magazine down and left the scene, hoping that whatever thoughts I was having would stay behind. But they did not.

For days, I was completely confused by these new realizations, but even as I was confused by them, it made me feel better to think them again. I went back to the magazine, and as I looked through the pages with a new perspective, my "third eye" began to open even further. Since the particular magazine I was looking at featured more "intimate" sexual encounters between men and women, I was, for the first time, exposed to images of sexual interactions between men and women. Even if Mom and Dad had tried to talk to me about sex, I was most likely unresponsive because I was either confused or just not ready, or both, but the magazine enlightened me to so many new realizations about myself.

At first, I found the new thoughts I was having very scary. I thought that I should have been looking at the pictures as if I were the man, being with the woman, but it was not that way at all. It was never that way. I even tried for years and years to see it from the man's perspective; still, I saw myself as the woman, every time. From then on, I realized that my sexuality was somehow askew: my sexual desires were based not on me being a boy or a man, with a girl or woman, but of me being a woman, and then being with a man. Talk about confusing! The other part of my brain, the part that is programmed by the social constructs of the world, constantly argued my newfound sexuality:

"You can't be a girl with a guy! That's ridiculous! It doesn't make sense!

"You are male, so you have to be with females!"

My other side would argue, "Oh right! But I'm a girl, and I want to be with guys!"

Confusion about this scary subject, shame for being different, guilt for hiding it, fear of potential consequences if others found out: all these feelings set in. Like concrete shoes, they fastened onto me, ready to pull me down into the darkest depressions I have ever known.

Something very derogatory and cruel that a family member once said to me over the phone affected me tremendously for a long time. It was a remark about my not dancing at my first junior high school dance. I was yelled at over the phone and called a very hurtful name. The experience was like a nail in the coffin of my shame and fear, and it proved to be a strong fuel to power more repression. In retrospect, I think I associated that attitude then with other people in my family, as well as with people in general. I learned firsthand how hurtful it was to be yelled at, or accused, for doing nothing wrong or for just being, so I turned inward and spent more and more time alone. My emotions were safer that way; being alone meant I wouldn't get hurt. But it surely didn't solve my problems.

Sometimes people say things that they don't think are all that big a deal, to them. But they often don't realize the kind of impact words can have on a person, especially on a child whose sense of self is as delicate and precarious as mine was. I have heard people say, "Oh, words are just words; they don't hurt anyone." That's utter crap. Words are incredibly powerful; they can be very uplifting or very sharp and damaging.

What Do You Want to Be when You Grow Up?

At some point during my early teens I was asked the all-too-popular question: "What do you want to be when you grow up?" Those asking the question were referring, of course, to what job did I want to do when I grow up. But the question impacted me differently. The only thing I could think was, "To be a girl." My reply, however, was, "Uh…I dunno." People would respond with a slight nod or just say oh. It was a moment like that, when what I felt inside came so critically close to the world outside, when I would become very scared. The fear would power the repression, and I would struggle to find ways to hide from the thoughts and feelings that I began to know were not going away. I tried to shuck them off as part of some kind of phase or temporary thing most guys must go through, but from what I could tell, none of my friends were going through anything remotely similar.

In terms of family, I was beginning to think that being a husband and father was what I was destined to be, but those thoughts seemed based not on the true me, but on something else. The thought that I should be living the role of a man felt so superficial. My subconscious was telling me something completely different, although I couldn't tell what it was exactly. I had occasional thoughts of being a wife and mother, although the notion perplexed me, considering the body I had. Any thoughts like that, with my confusion so deep and unforgiving, mostly led to more harsh repression and attempts to ignore the signs that constantly were trying to tell me something. Being accepted by my parents and friends weighed heavily on me. I kept telling myself that this thing in me was a phase; it would go away someday, and there really wasn't anything wrong with me. I was a decent-looking young man with a bright future, or so I thought! But I tried. I played the part my body imposed on me, that of the male, at least outwardly.

Do We All Feel the Same?
Do we all feel the same?
Do we all feel the same pain?
What I would give to never feel this way

...again
Twisting inside my brain
Burning every night and day
To let it go, let my soul fly away
...again
There's got to be so much more than this
There must be something more for me
There's got to be something more to life
Than drowning away in this misery

When the effects of testosterone began to move my body and mind into new, and very unwanted, directions, my emerging sexuality became a source of deepening confusion for me because on the one hand my sexual desire was as a female with a male, yet there I was, male. You know how it is when you want something and you just can't have it. You do your best to be near it as much as possible. Well, in many ways, that's what sex was for me. It was a confusing time for me, a roller-coaster ride of emotions. As my junior high and high school years ticked so slowly by, I became better acquainted with the physical parts of myself, although it wasn't easy. The more I realized that I was different from the women I saw in the world around me, the more frustrated and angry I became. Anger became a close friend of mine, for it was a pressure release valve for the thoughts and feelings I had been repressing for so long. My anger was also a mask to cover the real me that was trying harder and harder to break free of the walls of fear and to live her life. That was when the war in my head really began to intensify. When the frustration became overwhelming, it seemed easier to throw things, or smash stuff, like plastic models, drawings, or toys, than it was to deal with my growing incongruence. I must have appeared to be a very frustrated young man, smashing many of the things I owned. But as destructive as I could get at times, the opposite was also true, I was extremely creative with images, words, and ultimately music. Those three ways of expressing myself became channels into which I poured my heart and soul, right there for the world to see, and oddly enough, the world would never be the wiser as to what all those expressions actually meant!

War Torn

Been fighting this battle so long
I forgot which way is up
Two-sided conflict leaves me war torn One day, I pray, this
war will stop Detangle. Rearrange.
Dig in the trenches, bloody trenches
Defoliate the overgrowth inside the battle zone Destroy it all
'til one survives
Nobody else can see
This war inside of me
I'm dying for victory
Death is not an option
I'm bleeding inside—war torn
One has got to die—war torn
It's all inside—war torn
I must survive—war torn

My sole purpose during those mid- to-late-teen years was to overcome this bizarre twist of fate that was affecting my life so agonizingly. I just knew I could overcome it by suppressing it, or by ignoring it. But I'm here to tell you, it does not go away! So if you know someone who tells you that on inside he or she is the opposite of what you see on the outside, you should give serious consideration to what the person says, because there is no reason on earth a person would tell you that if it weren't true. Who would want to endure the things we, as transsexuals, have to go through just because we "want" to change our sex? No one! No, the transsexual condition is not about choice. It is a matter of fact that is etched into our lives when we are born. The only choice in the matter is what to do about it once we realize it and accept it. From my experience, and from that of the hundreds of trans people I have known throughout the years, there is no changing the mind. So that leaves us with only one option: change the body. And who with the transsexual condition wouldn't want to do what it takes to live a happy life?

It is interesting to observe the dichotomy of my situation in retrospect. Even though I tried hard to hide my true self, there were a few rare times when I let it out. One of those times was at the Halloween dance in my senior year of high school. My best friend, Tom, and I decided we were going to be girls for Halloween. Oddly, it was he who suggested it; I would never have even considered doing that, since I wanted so much to hide my feelings and especially because I would not want my peers to think I was some kind of freak. We elicited the help of two of our girl friends, Laura and Ruth. The four of us often spent time hanging out together, especially at lunch time in school. So the night of the dance, Tom and I rendezvoused with the girls at Laura's house. They helped us put on makeup, loaned us some clothes, and even helped us do our nails and hair. It was incredibly awesome for me; I loved every second of it. They expressed their amazement at how good I looked, and even though I relished their words, it scared me because I didn't want to appear to be "too good" at looking like a girl. I was just so afraid of being judged about who I really was.

The four of us piled into my car and headed toward the dance. Someone suggested that we stop at a quick mart to grab some gum, and that Tom and I should run in and get it. I pulled up in front of a Circle K, and Tom seemed too eager to get out and run in there. He hopped out of the car and tried to sashay into the store. He was so damn funny that we laughed our butts off in the car. Ruth and Laura told me to go on in there, and I went, too, but very reluctantly. There was a man behind the counter, the clerk, and he checked me out as I went in. I didn't know if he were looking at me because he thought I was a guy dressed as a girl, or because he thought I was cute. I had a picture of us from that night, and when I looked back at it a few years later, I remember thinking that if I had seen myself from another person's perspective, I would have thought I was a girl. That was extremely comforting!

Without incident, we left the Circle K and went to the dance, which was in our high school auditorium. As I had jokingly speculated, there was almost no one else wearing a costume. We waited in line, paid our dollars, and went in. The guy who took our money laughed at us, but not so much at us as with us, I guess. Tom was playing it up and being very silly. He was doing the opposite of trying to pass—making sure people knew he was a guy, I guess to avoid embarrassment. I was doing the opposite, though; I just wanted to blend in, to not be noticed, and especially to not be told that I was a guy. No one did, thank goodness.

We went into the gymnasium, and when we realized that there were only two or three other people wearing costumes (it was actually a night or two before Halloween), we started freaking out because then we knew that we would really stand out. I said, "Uh…dude, we can't be seen like this; there's no one else wearing a costume!" He agreed, and I suggested we hide under the bleachers until we figured out a plan. How funny that would have looked if someone had seen us hiding under there. We decided that it wasn't worth sticking around; besides, there weren't very many people there, and we didn't think any girls, except Ruth and Laura, would be very likely to dance with us, so we decided to bail. We told Ruth and Laura this, and Tom and I headed out. As scary as it was, it was a lot of fun, and I was glad we did it. The night affected me very, very deeply. It was a taste of who I could have been, who I *should* have been.

There Is No "Why," There Just Is

Toward the end of high school, I got my second job at one of the local popular fast-food chains. Our regional store supervisor would stop by once a month to check the calibration of the beverage machines and timers and to make sure the store was running smoothly. He was like clockwork, always on time and always making sure everything was running perfectly. One day, as he was testing the ratio of cola syrup to carbonated water, I asked about something related to what he was doing. In response, he said, "There is no 'why,' there just is." I don't know if it was a phrase he said often, or if this were the only time he had ever said those words to someone else, but little did he know how much he had affected me.

I responded with a contemplative "Oh…" and went back to the grill to continue making burgers. I thought about his comment and related it to my own life of confusion and incongruence, which was full-blown chaos for me at the volatile age of seventeen.

The impact those words had on me was as profound as was their simplicity. They have echoed in my mind almost every day since I heard them, and they have become my own response to many questions with no immediate answers. In many ways, I have lived my life by them; they have helped me to let go of futile attempts at understanding things that are impossible for me to comprehend, and they have helped teach me how to have patience with people, events, and things that are natural but incomprehensible. Things like transsexuality.

"There is no why, there just is" simply describes nature in its purest form. There is no explicit reason why a clover has three leaves; that's just the way it is, the way nature intended it, the way it evolved over millions of years. But it is not the only way it can be. It is just as natural, but far more rare, for a clover have four leaves. There is no reason why it's that way; it is just that way. It just happens. Like a four-leaf clover, I am what I am because I just am; because I exist. I was born this way, and I will die this way. It is my nature.

Another aspect of "there is no why, there just is" that I have learned to accept is the value of letting go. Let go of things in your head that just won't seem to go away because they have no definitive answers: curiosities, concerns, worries, and thoughts that occupy the mind and consume mental energy. Much of the time, most things are just not worth worrying about. You simply have to accept the fact that they are what they are, and there is nothing on earth you can do about them other than accept them. If you don't, you run the risk of depleting your mental energy fussing and worrying about them, and that energy is needed for living your life to its fullest.

Every day I had to remind myself that there is no reason why I was confused and incongruent; I just was. But that still didn't help me so much at the time. I knew that the problem I was having was far too deep and complex to just ignore, so I spent a lot of time trying to figure out exactly what was wrong with me. During those times, I hid it well and repressed it so well that no one, not even Mom and Dad, knew I had issues.

Don't?
With pain comes resurrection
Fear brings blind infection
Pleasure is the completion
Hatred is the deletion
Black is the soul of the damned
Black is the color of night
Black is the caressing void
Black is what I am
Don't come near me; don't question me
Don't touch me; don't answer me
Don't look at me; don't talk about me
Don't listen to me; don't think about me
You fear what I suggest, you fear what I am
With life comes resurrection
Pleasure breeds infection
Death is the completion
Death is the deletion
Dead is the soul of the damned
Dead is the color of night
Dead is the caressing void

Dead is what I am

Another phrase that has had an equally monumental impact on my life was one that Dad used to tell me at least once every time we went hiking together: "A constant dripping wears away stone."

I remember seeing many a boulder in a stream or creek that proved this concept. Over the years, as water dripped or poured down onto the stone, a dip or hole had developed where the water hit the rock. Slow, repetitive, and persistent dripping over the course of many years, even decades, had washed tiny pieces of the rock away, leaving what looked like a bowl carved into the stone. Many of these bowls even had small troughs that had been etched by the water as it had flowed through, making a natural pouring channel for directing the water on down using the path of least resistance.

Dad would remind me of this, usually several miles into the hike, when I would be getting tired and would start complaining that my back, legs, or feet were sore. I would ask how far it was "'til we get there."

"A constant dripping wears away stone, kiddo," he would always say.

"Yeah, well, my feet are killing me…My back hurts. Can't we just stop here and rest?" I would say.

I watched him ahead of me, with his huge orange pack loaded with everything we needed for survival. It was so big that it obscured his head and shoulders, and all I could see were his arms and legs, walking stick in one hand, the other hand sometimes holding his sweat-soaked bandana. His pace was always steady and solid, and I would contemplate what he said as I watched him. I would try to understand those words, but usually drifted off into thoughts about other things. It took me some time before I really understood how that phrase implied the idea that patience and persistence worked together as one to achieve a goal. When I finally understood this, some years later, I realized that I had already been applying it to myself. Then I realized that someday, no matter what happened, I would find myself and would become whole and congruent.

Destiny and Human Reason

Webster's Dictionary defines fate as "the principle or determining cause or will by which things in general are believed to come to be as they are or events to happen as they do: DESTINY."

Many of us believe in destiny—we believe there is a power or force that causes the inevitable to happen, and that our lives are intrinsically tied to this mysterious power. For all human beings, the concept of destiny plays a huge role in our lives, whether we believe that our lives are preordained or that we are in full control of the outcomes of our own decisions. Interestingly, there is a strong human element that appears to get in the way of a complete openness or willingness to accept our own destiny and go with our own flow: reason.

Human reason, or the assumption of it, often seems to influence our choices in life. We often over think things to such a degree that the crux of what we seek to resolve in our lives becomes vague and almost imperceptible. We lose ourselves and our natural inclinations amid the sometimes self-manipulating effects of our own intellect and thinking.

When dealing with such intrinsic issues as transsexualism, those of us who are dealing with it personally seem to have an inherent ability to over think, to over reason about who we are until we've intellectually ruled out the feasibility of our true selves. Our reasoning minds, fed during our lifetimes by the social constructs in which we live, obstruct our ability to see ourselves, and our own natures, clearly and without societal clutter. We tend to try to justify everything we are feeling. For example, when I was in the early stages of trying to understand myself I thought, "I want to be female. I should have been born female." But my reasoning mind would respond with something like, "Yeah, but you were born male, so you have to be male. There's no such thing as having a female brain in a male body. If you were meant to be female, you would have been born female!" This easily becomes an endless loop of self-argument, where feeling and thinking are in complete and utter opposition, and it stems from what we learn as we grow up in our social surroundings. Often the things we learn are not even blatantly pronounced or said out loud; they are inferred in the subtlest of ways. A good example of this is the assumption that because a person is male that they are required to be the primary financial provider of the household, or that they are the one who is supposed to be the initiator when it comes to things like sex. Our masculine and feminine roles are well-defined by the advertising we see, hear and read, and by the movies and television we watch. Regardless, we know that we feel female, but we consciously think that it isn't possible we could actually be female within a male body.

In a very real sense, we obscure that which we know to be true about ourselves with that which we have learned throughout our lives. We know we should have been female from the very inception of our lives, yet we have learned that changing sex is wrong, or immoral, or that it is some kind of perversion or somehow only related to the physical act of having sex. Stereotypes and assumptions abound, and the more shocking an explanation is, the more the world talks about it. Unfortunately, this often breeds more misconceptions. There's not so much excitement in the fact that some people are born with gender-opposing brain and body combinations. People who do not understand what it is like make it out to be much more incredible than it really is. It's just not that big of a deal.

The true "problem" with transsexuality is not the condition itself, it is the method by which non-transsexuals generally handle the subject: often with sensationalism and obfuscation, emotional responses that come with the territory of the uneducated or compassionless.

Churn

This life, not all it seems
Gets me off the greatest extreme
On and off my mind goes
With night and day my anger grows
Spilling hate into a street of lies
Their words cut through me like razor-bladed lies
Churn it out to seek the lobe
Mankind is what he doesn't know

A product of his own devise
He turns to face a world of lies
A grand façade—a world of clay
He reaps his sow while he decays
At the end we're all the same
Earth our sad ball and chain
And everything we do—our quest for clay
Could it all just be a whirlwind in vain?

There are so many factors that shape our human reason. Today, there are incredible amounts of incoming data that we must digest—from our parents and grandparents, religious and spiritual teachings, books, movies, television, radio, Internet, friends' opinions, family traditions, and word of mouth. The list is long, and I'm sure you can think of many other sources. It is tough for those of us who are different to deal with all of this. Our lives become entrenched in the self-enclosed battle of who we are versus who the world expects us to be, because who we are goes against the grain of what is considered normal in our society. As young adults we are perplexed not only by the usual fare—puberty, graduating high school, and trying to figure out what we want to do with our lives— but also we have to figure out just who we are in the first place.

So we are left with our selves alone to try to figure it out. This is the saddest thing of all and one of the main reasons why we feel so isolated, so alone. We think that each of us is the only one in the entire universe who could be so unduly messed up. We become extremely confused, and we seclude ourselves from our own lives. Why live a life that isn't our own? Why bother being the best we can be if we can't even be ourselves? This can lead to all sorts of escapism through drugs, alcohol, and negative behavior toward ourselves, toward those with whom we live, and toward the world in general. Oftentimes, since we do not understand who, or why, we are, we take it out on the ones we assume to be responsible: our parents. But they are not responsible for our being different. No one is responsible for anyone else's unique disposition in life. It is what it is, and it is just one of the many variances of life itself. It's not that we are different; it's how we deal with being different. We need to learn to accept ourselves and love ourselves for who and what we are. The only way to do that is through education—for ourselves and for others. The world needs to understand that we are natural, that we are okay, and that we are not freaks. This is happening, ever so slowly, but it is happening.

So often we find ourselves trapped between what we know is true about ourselves and what our reason dictates should be the truth. We entertain the idea of changing our bodies to conform to our minds because we know that there is no changing our minds. But then we place ourselves in the context of our world, our lives, and our families, and we do not see how it could be possible for us to change. We become dismayed by the thoughts; we become depressed because we do not see a way to be happy in this world by being ourselves. We fear we won't be accepted. We repress our thoughts, and we hide ourselves from ourselves through more repression, drugs, or other means. We try to ignore it. We try to excuse it. We try to wish it away. You name it—we've tried it. But, there's no getting away from it. Some who have realized this have been so afraid of the possibilities of change that they have taken the most permanent way out of their plight by taking their own lives. There is absolutely, positively no reason for this. There may be a rare number of circumstances in which ending your own life is a viable option, but the transsexual condition is not one of them.

Education is the foundation of change. In order to change something, anything, people need to be educated. In order for us to accept ourselves, to change our lack of acceptance of who we are, we must first learn about who we are. This is tough when what we are trying to learn about is so cryptic and obscure. It's a very hard to define a way of being. It is more of a feeling than anything else, for it is not something obvious to us. As more research has been done on the subject, it appears that transsexualism is, for lack of a more scientific definition, quite literally a female brain in a male body. Even with this knowledge and data to back it up, there is still no tangible proof; we cannot see it with our eyes, cannot touch it with our fingertips, and cannot hear it except in the thoughts in our heads that arise from the feelings deep within us that something is inherently different with us. Thus we cannot "prove" to others that this is who we are, until after we start to change. People have a very hard time accepting things they cannot see, especially with regard to this situation. When it becomes obvious to them that something is being done, or has been done, then they are more apt to accept it and move on to the next phase of coping or understanding.

One of the most important levels of change that needs to happen with regard to transsexual education is on the public front. As trans individuals, we can educate ourselves pretty well these days, because we are seeking out specific information. The pressing issue is closing the gap, getting the people who don't think about this subject matter to learn and to understand. We need television to stop portraying us as "men in dresses," and we need the idiotic stereotyping to cease. We need people to stop saying things like, "She used to be a man." I did not "used to be" a man. I used to be male. I never was a man, but I did a good job acting like one. We need to raise awareness that this is a medical condition, not a mental one. Sure, it has something to do with our minds, but don't all medical conditions affect our mental faculties?

We, as transsexuals, need to be less afraid of people knowing about us and our situations. This is hard for those who have not yet transitioned to their proper gender, and I would not even recommend that they be too open about it until after they transition. But for those of us who have transitioned, it is vitally important for us to be open about who we are and what we've had to deal with in our lives. We are the best educators on the subject, for we have lived the subject; we are the subject.

This isn't an easy thing for us to do, even for me. It's been a hard decision to make—coming out and not just living a life of stealth. But when I think about how alone and isolated I felt as a kid, as a teenager, as a young adult in my twenties, and even as an adult during my thirties, and when I realize that right now there are hundreds, thousands, even tens of thousands of people living with this situation…well, I just can't imagine not trying to help in some way. Something is better than nothing, even if it means putting myself on the line.

What to do? If you are in the throes of dealing with this condition and you are reading this book, then you are taking the first steps toward change. Congratulations! That is sometimes the hardest thing to do! If you feel isolated and alone, know that you are most definitely not the only one in the world feeling the way you do. There is always someone else who has been through what you're going through. My advice at this point is that if you have not done so already, find a support group; I also suggest that you find a good psychologist or counselor to speak to who is compassionate with regard to transsexual issues. There are many of them, and one of the best resources for up-to-date contact information is the Internet.

Most importantly, don't get down on yourself for being this way. Don't let your "reason" judge you. Don't be afraid to accept who you are. Take a deep breath and let your true self be expressed. Give yourself and the world the best gift that you could give—you.

I suspect that one of the main reasons we don't come out of the closet in our teens, to the world or even to ourselves, is because we are so afraid of the backlash from our peers. We fear their lack of acceptance. We fear reprisals: the teasing and harsh accusations that will be directed at us because we don't fit the mold. And we fear physical harm. Who wants to be beaten up for being honest and truthful about being different than the norm? It doesn't really matter what it is that is different from the norm; it could be anything. If you stand out from the crowd for any reason, you risk ostracism, or even physical and emotional harm. As part of my defense mechanism, I turned my efforts in the direction opposite of who I really was. I donned the "tough guy" attitude, not blatantly, but somehow subtly so that, for some weird reason, the bullies at school never bothered me after fifth grade. Maybe it was my skill at blending in, maybe it was the look in my eyes that said, "Don't fuck with me!" But I always figured that I had been through more pain than they could ever dole out, so I welcomed the chance to beat the hell out of them, if for nothing else than to release my pent-up frustrations. It was never in my character to initiate anything like that. Funny how we adapt.

To cope with all of this pressure from the outside, we tend to master the art of repression, subconsciously feeling that to avoid pain, it is better to hide who we really are from the world and from ourselves. As we repress our most intrinsic needs and desires, we endeavor to appear as normal as the other people in our social arena. The ironic thing about this whole situation is that most of those other people in our social arena are very likely struggling to fit in with the norm as much as we are, for any number of different reasons. In this effort, we adopt the expected behaviors of the norm, and we become the world's greatest actors, living the play of life by the terms of what is set or expected by our immediate or larger society. As is often the case, we begin this journey of self-obscuration during our most mentally, emotionally, and sexually formative years—our teens. In so doing, we become entrenched in a routine that we believe will keep us safe and secure; however, we lack the experience and foresight to be able to realize the consequences of our actions. This, I believe, is the root of my misunderstanding of my own sexuality; yet there are still some unresolved issues I am compelled to explore.

One can only repress one's true feelings and true self for so long before something gives. It's a lot like putting air in a balloon. The air going into the balloon is our repression. In those moments when we feel the "unwanted" or "undesirable" feelings or thoughts, we push them down, deep within our brains, like blowing a breath of air into the balloon. The more we repress, the more that balloon fills, and the harder it gets for us to blow more air into it. Eventually the balloon reaches its threshold of resistance, and it blows up. The resulting explosion of emotion can manifest itself in various negative ways, including anger, rage, alcoholism, drug addiction, food addiction, and even suicide. The only feasible solution, in any case, is to cease blowing the air into the balloon, to stop repressing, and to let out all the extra air so that the balloon can reach its natural state of equilibrium. If we do not stop repressing, and do not begin dealing with our issues in a constructive and positive manner, then we will most likely be heading for disaster. That is very sad when you consider the fact that it would be so easy to deal with things, if only we had the desire to, or could get over our fears.

Some people are better at repressing feelings of transsexualism than others. I think one reason for this is the state of the world when we grow up, and the particular attitudes of the general social arena in which we live. At the time of this writing, there appear to be many more young transsexuals dealing more openly with their issues than there are older transsexuals dealing with their issues in an open way. I believe this is because of the way the social views of gays, lesbians, and transgendered people are perceived in our popular culture. Even thirty years ago, all of these topics were scorned by the majority of people in our society. With my limited exposure to social conduct and attitudes, it is hard for me to say just how far we've come in the past thirty years, but certainly there has been some very good progress. Unfortunately there are certain political and religious forces that are working very hard to undo all the progress that has been made in this regard. That, I find, is a very sad thing. Why would people want to limit people, for any reason, but especially for just being true to who they are? That just does not seem fair. No one has the right to tell another that they don't have a right to live the life that they've been given.

As is often the case with transsexuals, especially male-to-female trans women, we struggle internally for years and years trying to manage our feelings. Inside, we know who we really are and who we really want, or need, to be. But outwardly we are not true to ourselves. This often happens because of social expectations, but it also happens because of our own nature. We do have male bodies, and we do look like men. We ask ourselves, "How the hell can I change all this?" and we do not have even a clue how to answer the question.

Add to all this internal conflict and confusion the fact that many of us repress the feelings as much as we possibly can. Often, it is much easier to repress, to push away or hide from ourselves, the feelings we have that make us hurt. We don't want to hurt; we just want to be happy, to live in peace, and to be loved for who we are. To be loved is one of the most important things in the entire world to us—how could someone else possibly love us if we are so twisted, so freakish, so wrong? The world around us, which has no idea what kind of inner turmoil we are dealing with, has literally said nothing to us directly about our feelings, yet we tell ourselves that we are freaks, perverts, wrong, or morally doomed because of our feelings.

It is often the love relationships that we build with our closest partner, our lover, our best friend, our soul mate, our wife whom we fear losing the most. We often spend years and years building the perfect marriage, doing for our spouse all the things we know will please her, often, because we know those things would please us. We put all her needs and desires before our own, and we tell ourselves that we would die for her! Indeed, we *are* dying for her. Is that what she would really want if she knew?

This seems to be common thread among a majority of transsexual women— we seem to think that having a family and being a father will help squelch or "cure" our true feelings. In thinking that having a family and raising children will make our incongruent feelings go away, we entrench ourselves in a futile rut fraught with the perils of emotional and physical problems. We turn to things such as food, drugs, or other forms of self-abuse or addiction as a distraction. Somewhere along the line we lose our sense of self-worth. The value we place on our self declines with every thought repressed, and depression creeps ever deeper into our lives. Because we are trying so desperately to hide who we are, especially from our spouse and immediate family, we struggle also to hide our depression over it, often acting out in other ways just to purge ourselves of the inner anguish that is snowballing within us. Ultimately, we reach the threshold of resistance and something must happen—whether it is of our own conscious choice, or expressed in a physical or emotional response. Life naturally follows the path of least resistance, and if the path of least resistance leads to the popping of the proverbial balloon, then watch out! It is vital to our well-being, vital to our very existence that we deal head on with the things that have driven us to such repressive behavior.

There really is only one answer to this problem: change. We *must change*! First of all, we must admit to ourselves that we have issues that must be confronted and must be handled *immediately*. Second of all, we must *stop repressing* these issues! Thirdly, we must admit to ourselves that *we cannot handle this on our own*, and we must avail ourselves of the support of others who are familiar with the situation we are facing. We must *seek outside help*! Without it, we lessen our chances for survival.

Coming to terms with transsexualism is not an easy task for many different reasons, not the least of which is the fact that it seems so surreal and incomprehensible. In reality, it is a very subjective experience. There is no way to quantify it or show it to others, not even to ourselves. All our lives, we tell ourselves that what we're feeling isn't real, that it must be some kind of phase, or that we must just be cross-dressers or something—anything that is somehow easier for our minds to grasp. For most of us, it takes years, sometimes decades, of living with the feelings before we finally admit to ourselves that we are dealing with a real and present situation. But once we do, and we have finally begun confronting the issues at hand, we have reached the first step in dealing with our long-fought feelings.

The only way to stop repressing our feelings is to admit to ourselves that we have issues that need to be resolved in the best way possible. This "best way possible" is rather vague, though, and is really based on the individual. What is of the utmost importance, however, is that we actually do make the proper adjustments in order to live happy and fulfilling lives. Often, we have weighed these options over and over in our minds during the years of suppressing: "What if I really did change my sex? How would my spouse feel?" or "What would my family think?" or "What would my co-workers, my friends, my child's parents, think of me?" And to our own detriment, we superimpose our own fears onto the imagined responses of the people in our lives. We imagine, and then we assume the worst of all possible outcomes. Why? What do we have to base these assumptions on? First-hand experience? Not usually. Second-hand experience? Not very likely. Often we fear the worst possible outcomes because of the sensationalism of transsexuals in the media, especially tabloid television, which exploits us in many ways, to increase their ratings and their profits.

We don't often realize it, but our media, including local and national news, specialty news shows, and sensationalistic television talk shows all have a tendency to focus on the negative aspects of any topic. When it comes to the topic of transsexualism, over the years the subject has been fraught with extreme sensationalism and outright negative publicity. We have been treated as freaks, clowns and perverts with blatant disregard of the human beings we are. This has done nothing positive to support compassion and understanding of those dealing with the transsexual condition, and it has had a very negative impact on the way society generally perceives us. The main reason is because we, the real human beings who are portrayed so wrongly on many shows, hide ourselves from the world. If only we could overcome our fear, fight for ourselves and for our fellow transsexual men and women, stand up, be out, be proud, and make a difference! Then, when ridiculous television shows attempt to

sensationalize us and make us look bad, the world at large will know, first or second hand, that these shows are full of crap. It's a long, slow, arduous process, but this is the main reason I am open about who I am and where I come from. But we must all get over it and be willing to be visible and available to help others.
Unfortunately for most of us, taking on the challenges of this condition is nearly too overwhelming. Many of us face an incredible array of problems that must be solved, and each problem solved has far-reaching consequences that can themselves introduce new problems in our lives. For example, what if we do decide to change our sex? What then do we, as one half of the couple equation, do? Do we stay with our spouse? Do we want to stay with our spouse? Does our spouse want to stay with us after we have become the opposite sex? Interestingly, there are an amazing number of spouses who are sticking it out and staying together. Several of the transsexual women who had surgery in Canada when I went have spouses that were there with them, and are still with them today. I have talked to many transsexual women during the past two years whose spouses are staying with them. That is an amazing and wonderful thing. But these are transsexual women who still have sexual desire for women, so it works out. What I don't fully understand is how their spouses, who married men, could make lesbian relationships work. But there are many things I am not meant to understand, and I will leave it to them to explain that part of the story.

The Question of Sex

While sexuality and sexual preference seem to be an unchanging factor for most people, they have been huge and often deeply confusing issues for me—especially considering that my sexual preference, is for men *[At the time I wrote this. It has since changed.]*, and that I was deeply in love with, and married to, a woman for thirteen years. Now, after years of study, I think I more fully understand what the term bisexual means, and funny as it might seem, I guess I, and others like me, are the ultimate in "bi" sexuality.

The crux of my struggle for sexual identification started when I was in my early teens, as puberty hit me, my body started changing, and sexual desires began to emerge. My gender identity began to emerge prior to my body's pubescent physical changes; that worked well for me in some ways because my body, while male, was not quite as masculine as it would be after puberty, so at the time I felt more normal than I did after hair began growing on my chest and other secondary sexual traits began to emerge. With the onset of puberty, and the beginning signs of masculinization, it seemed as though my sexual desires were those of a completely different person, wholly unrelated to the person I was beginning to see in the mirror. In my fantasies and dreams, I was female, and I was engaging in sexual acts with a male in what is considered straight sex. If it were not for the shape of my body at the time, and its increasingly boyish appearance, it might not have seemed so strange to be thinking that way. However, since I had the body of what, to me, was the opposite sex, compared to the image of myself in my mind, I didn't understand it at all, and I became incredibly confused. I could not empathize with my male friends, who were beginning to express sexual desires for girls, although I did not have desires for my male friends. I was in a kind of sexual limbo, created by growing confusion about who I was. The dissonance I would feel so intensely later in life was beginning to grow within me, and I became alienated from my male friends. That's not to say that I abandoned all of them, but it became increasingly hard to relate to them, especially when they would talk about girls in derogatory or demeaning ways. As a young (and confused) person, it was simply impossible for me to stand up for the girls they berated—my friends would never have understood, and I did not want to embarrass myself. In many ways, I always felt as though I were hanging on to my social life by a thin and quickly fraying thread.

Dating became something I did mostly because it was fun, because I was attracted to girls, but also because it was a way of getting closer to myself, in a vicarious kind of way. I dated a few girls here and there, went to movies, kissed, had sex, and was mostly thrilled with the fact that I could actually touch a woman's body, instead of just thinking about having my own. During sex, I began a process of transposition. I would imagine myself as her. My ability to do that improved over time, and it became something I needed to satisfy the growing realization that what I wanted out of sex was to be the woman, with a man. Complete confusion and incongruence ensued, which ultimately fueled my determination to find answers to my questions.

Hear Me Scream
I've lost my head again
And lost my only friends
The end is closing in
I slip in...to nothing
And now it is too late to ever go back
What I thought: confusion—what I couldn't see
Now standing on the edge, trails of broken glass
Reflections through blood of all I once did be
And I pick up a handful of glass and blood
The bits of my life drip through my fingertips
Coagulation clogs up the cracks in my mind
Squeezing hard on handfuls of glass as reality slips
Into a void all blue and cold and frozen
Thought I was waking up into a dream
But my eyes were fixed on something.
Nothing.
There was nobody there to hear me scream.

Still, there were no answers. How could there be answers when I couldn't even formulate the questions? I had no idea what was going on inside me, so there was no way I could pose the question other than, "What the hell is wrong with me!?" All I knew was that I wasn't gay, and that my problem was much more complicated than that. In an effort to avoid, and in order to cope with these feelings, I turned to music.

Music — An Emotional Release

Music was almost instantly something in which I could completely lose myself. One of the first songs I remember, and to this day I still remember exactly where I was when I heard it, was "American Pie," by Don McLean. "Drove my Chevy to the levy but the levy was dry..." I will never forget it. I was sitting in the back seat of Mom and Dad's early 1970s Ford Maverick, leaning forward (there were no seatbelt requirements in those days) on the middle of the big brown vinyl seat, between the headrests. The two of them in the front seat, Dad driving, as we cruised through Philadelphia. Dad was singing along with the chorus, and we were having one of those silly family moments. The memory will never fade. The power of music is phenomenal. When I hear that song, it instantly whisks me back to that moment.

A serious interest in music started for me when I was in my very early teens, even though I had tried the coronet when I was in the fourth or fifth grade. During the evenings, my parents and I would watch television together in our living room. Mom and Dad would sit in their chairs at the back of the room; Mom was usually knitting or sewing, and Dad was usually drawing or reading. I would lie right in the middle of the room, either

Christmas 1980

on the floor with a pillow or on a big brown or blue beanbag. I don't remember exactly which show it was that I saw him on, but I will never forget the experience. I lay there staring at the TV as a strange, orange haired person's face filled the screen. Was it a man or a woman? I couldn't tell; whoever it was had on a lot of makeup. It could have been either male or female.

As it turned out, it was Ziggy Stardust (David Bowie), and as he performed, I watched in awe and wonder, with my jaw and eyes as wide open as they could be. It was a turning point in my life. The power of his image floored me (good thing I was already on the floor!), and the music and his voice…well, I cannot assemble words enough to describe how all of that made me feel. All I remember is being drawn in and blown away, and then asking Mom and Dad, "Who was that?" I had never seen anything like it before, and all I wanted from then on was to see him perform again.

Ziggy might have made it back to our television after that, but I don't remember when. It almost didn't matter, though, because it wasn't long after seeing Ziggy that I was blessed with the eye and ear candy of another amazing television performance that totally changed my life forever. The scene was the same: me on beanbag, folks in chairs. I don't know which show it was, maybe *Saturday Night Live* or *Live at the BBC*, but this time the screen was filled with black-and-white painted faces. The people looked like evil clowns, but cooler. They looked like demons, aliens, and cats. Their hair was black and long. They wore black leather and spikes. But it wasn't just the visuals; it was the music, too. When I heard their guitars and the drums, and they burst into a full-blown show, my head was spinning with excitement. Thoughts about everything else in my life disappeared, and I left this earth altogether in a splendid euphoria of rock and roll. Who I was and wasn't didn't matter all of a sudden. My problems and confusion disappeared, and after what seemed like mere seconds, they were done. It was at that very moment that I realized I couldn't do anything else; I knew what I had to do with my life. I had to rock!

I spent a lot of my spare time with KISS records on my turntable, listening to them all night with headphones on. I began to realize how many rock bands there were, and that most, if not all, the guys had long hair; I had found something really special. First, the music moved me in ways I had never known. There was such a power there. I wanted to make others feel the feeling I had when I listened to that music. Plus, I wanted to let my hair grow long and have a good excuse for it. So I started playing guitar, which has grown into a life-long passion I will always cherish.

My first guitar was actually Mom's classical guitar. She took me to the local music store because she was buying a guitar to use in her classroom (she was an elementary school teacher). I sat down on the floor in front of a maroon Gibson SG, with which I had desperately fallen in love. So much so, that I later took my camera down there and shot a bunch of pictures of it! But Mom wouldn't buy me the SG. She told me I should start learning on her classical guitar first; that disappointed me tremendously because I really wanted to make some noise. But I tried it anyway, and I am very glad I did.

The vibrations of the guitar boomed into my right ear like thunder, as I rested my head down on the wide body of the guitar. I plucked the low E and A strings, and fretted some simple chords as I listened to the heavy sound, distorted by the proximity of my ear on the rosewood. It was an amazing sound, full and rich with overtones and rough vibrations, distorted by its own resonance in the wood. As the sound vibrated my skull, it warmed my soul, and I could swear that for even just the briefest moment I was numb to all that felt so wrong in my world. I thought, too, that maybe, somehow, this vibration, like a drug of some kind, could somehow magically massage away the ever-growing dissonance I felt within my own being. I embraced the sound with my soul as I embraced the guitar with my body, and I sat there for the longest time, just listening to the beautiful tones of a single, low E note.

To my amazement, I felt much better after doing that, and so it was that my heart and soul became truly soothed by the healing power of music. Funny, even now, at nearly forty years old, I still lay my head down on the side of one of my acoustic guitars and let the vibrations soothe my soul. I have come such a long way, but there are some things, like music, that will never change.

Eventually, Mom decided to give me that guitar, and I will never forget that day. I was in the front living room of our house, by the library, which was an entire wall filled with books. I picked up the guitar, about to take it upstairs to my room, when she told me I could have it. I was so thrilled! Then was when I really began to practice on it, trying to play some KISS and AC/DC stuff, but it did not have the powerful sound of the electric guitars that I wanted to make.

After sitting and pondering the sound of electric guitars, and trying to figure out how they work, an idea dawned on me: the sound of the side of the classical guitar sure did sound a lot like a loud electric guitar! A plan started to take root. The first thing I tried was putting the microphone of my little boom box inside the guitar's sound hole…and I mean literally putting it inside. That didn't work very well. It sounded like crap, and the wire coming out of the sound hole was in the way of my picking hand. So, I sat and pondered some more. "Hmm…" My wheels were turning. I had some old, broken cassette player parts handy, one part of which was a 3-inch speaker. I knew microphones were basically the same as speakers, and I thought that guitar pickups must be similar to them as well, so the solution hit me!

I taped the 3-inch speaker to the top of the guitar, out of the way of my hand. Then I cut the microphone off its wire and attached the wires to the speaker. After that, I inserted the plug into my boom box mic input. I turned it on and played the guitar—and was amazed to hear a sound much like an electric guitar!

It wasn't long after that Mom and Dad bought me my first real electric guitar and an old Fender Twin Reverb amplifier. I kept practicing and started getting together with other guitar players. The more I practiced, the more I began to find a place where I felt as if I fit in: a place for outcasts, for guys who wanted to let their hair grow long, and for those who broke away from social norms. The music, the image, and the lifestyle all carried a huge fascination for me, and I immersed myself in it.

Ever since I began playing guitar, twenty-three years ago, I have been through so much in just a musical sense. It is amazing how much a person can evolve, both within and in social contexts, with music as an integral part of who you are and what you do.

During my senior year in high school, I got my first band going with a friend of mine, Shannon, who played drums. His friend, Rich, joined us on bass. Rich had never played bass before, so he was quite green, but it didn't matter much because I had only been playing for a few months myself. Shannon had more experience than Rich and I combined, but he was still very green, too.

The first song we started playing together was "Livin' After Midnight," by Judas Priest. It was a pretty easy song to play, a straightforward rocking tune, but we didn't have anyone to do the singing for us. I couldn't sing at all, so I wouldn't do it seriously, but I did yell out the words just to try to make it more fun. We learned some more Priest stuff like "Breakin' the Law," and a few other metal songs, but that was about it. We never performed as a band because we were all in such an early phase of our own learning. It's actually hard to get a band together when you're still in the early learning phases of being a musician. Being in a band is a whole new thing. But I think it also just depends on the people involved. We had a lot of fun.

One day, the three of us set our gear up at Rich's parents' new house during the middle of winter. It was so cold and snowing outside. Rich's parents were building their new house on the side of a long, sloping hill on their property. Since the house was still under construction, it was a large cinderblock formation, with one wall completely open to the canyon outside. The living room was a slab of concrete, three walls, and a roof. We set our gear up out there while it was snowing, and we played for an hour or so. By the time we stopped, my fingers were so cold I literally could not move them! They had become numb, and I couldn't even open the latch on my guitar case. When we clambered up the hill to their other house, I had my guitar in one hand and my case in the other. I thought for sure my fingers were going to break off like icicles.

After I graduated from high school, the three of us went our separate ways. Shannon hooked up with another guitar player, Tony, who was another musician friend of mine. I seem to recall contacting him based on an ad he had put up at the local music store. He was one of those gifted guitar players, who back then at the age of about fourteen, had learned the entire Ratt album *Out of the Cellar* in less than a day, solos and all. He was quite an inspiration for me, though I don't think I ever told him that. Recently, I found out that he's still playing and still in a number of bands. Perhaps he'll read this and learn that he inspired me to play more. It's amazing how many people we interact with during our lives that inspire us to better ourselves in one way or another, and yet we often don't even realize that they have, let alone thank them for it.

Shannon and Tony formed a good band that played some good cover material, like "Wild Side" by Motley Crue. Shannon could tear up some Tommy Lee drumming! I watched those guys play a couple of years later and was simply amazed at the intricacy and dynamics of their playing. I haven't heard from Shannon since then. It's been about twenty years, I think, and I've often wondered where he ended up, and whether or not he's still playing.

I enrolled at Arizona State University in 1984, and I was there for almost a year. Mom and Dad paid for it, and I ended up blowing it. I was very sorry about that for many years, but I can't say that I really regret the choices I made, although I wish now that I had stuck with school. But if I had, I might never have met Cindy, and that would mean that Anvil wouldn't be here. So, all-in-all, I'm glad things worked out the way they did. Even though I have apologized for ruining their expectations of me that year, I find that my father still has a hard time with it. In fact, we were talking about the past recently, and when this topic came up, his head turned almost as red as a tomato and he became very upset. I thought he was going to blow his top! It has been nearly twenty years. I had hoped he would have forgiven me by now, or at least gotten over it, but from his reaction it is apparent that he has not. Why they thought I would do well in college when I completely sucked at all my other schools is beyond me. Even I didn't think I would do very well, but I hoped it would be different. I hoped it would be easier. Little did I know how incredibly challenging it would be, not only in scholastic terms, but in having to deal with my personal situation as my problem grew.

I lived in a dorm room on the ASU campus, with one male roommate who wasn't around very often. I played a lot of guitar then. My major was music, and I was taking private classical guitar lessons as well. At the time, I didn't have a job, and the few extra dollars I got from Mom and Dad sometimes didn't last too long. My friend and I lived on fifty-nine cent, fast-food burgers on weekends (we had prepaid cafeteria access during the week), and I even found sustenance in the form of ketchup packets from time to time. In order to make a few quick bucks for food and guitar picks or strings, I found myself going to the local blood plasma center and selling plasma, for which I got paid ten dollars each time. It was not a fun experience, having your blood drawn out and the blood cells put back in with cold saline. It was quite gross, actually. I only did it several times. Interestingly, I had forgotten until very recently about a transsexual woman who used to go in there all the time. In fact, she was in there almost every time I was. I can almost remember her name; the nurse said it quite often. One day I sat next to her in the waiting area. I still remember what her nails looked like. At the time, I thought she was kind of weird, but at the same time I felt that she and I were somehow kindred spirits. That was when I was eighteen, which was long before I really understood transsexualism or gender issues. I figured she had been a man at one point in her life, but I had no clue whatsoever what she must have been through to get where she was when our paths crossed. Her presence didn't bother me at all, but I was very intrigued. I wonder now what would have happened if I had been able to express my feelings to her, or ask her about herself. I wonder what direction my life would have taken.

My first semester started off well enough, but I quickly fell behind in my classes. I had way too many personal issues that got in the way of my ability to think clearly at any given moment, so I turned to the one thing that had been a release and escape for me—music. I decided that I should get into, or start up, a band. I began to advertise for band mates, which I found rather quickly.

A guy named Randy, who played bass and guitar, lived in the dorm building next to mine. We met through an ad one of us had posted on a dorm bulletin board; we got together and started working on some songs. We found a singer and a drummer, neither of whom attended ASU, and pretty soon we had enough songs to play a full set of music. We called the band Craz. It was pronounced "craze," but I always thought it read as though the "a" sounded the way it does in the word "apple."

Most of our practices took place off campus, but there were a few times when we would set up and play in our dorm. During spring break, almost everyone was gone from the dorms, and we decided to take some acid and set up our gear in Randy's dorm room, which had space for three people to live. We shoved everything back against the back wall and set up our gear, aiming it at the front door and windows. Then we turned up our amps as loud as they would go and played through our set.

It didn't take long before the dorm administrator came by to tell us to turn it off. He yelled at us to turn it down, and we just kept on playing and yelling at him, "What?" and "Huh?" and giving him a hard time. When he finally said, "You guys turn it off or get kicked out of the dorms!" we turned it off. We laughed about that day for a long time!

As time went on, and the notion that I was going to become a famous guitar player became greater and greater in my mind, I decided that I needed to devote more time to practicing and less to other things—school, in particular. Shortly after the second semester started, I had completely stopped going to class. I did, however, still go to the cafeteria to use my student ID to get "free" lunches. My daily routine was like this:

5:30 AM—Get up.

6:00 AM—Go to cafeteria and eat breakfast.

6:30 AM—Return to dorm; practice guitar until 11:30 AM.
11:30AM—Put guitar down; go eat lunch.

12:30 PM—Return to dorm; practice guitar until 5:30 PM.
5:30 PM—Go to cafeteria; eat dinner.

6:15 PM—Return to dorm; practice guitar until whenever.

10:00 PM–12:00 AM—Fall asleep on bed.

I usually fell back and stared at the ceiling as I played, then fell asleep. I'd wake up a while later and put my guitar in its case.

That was literally my schedule for about five months. I was so committed to improving my skills that I even used masking tape on my dorm window to write my motto, "Play 'til they bleed!" But no matter how hard I tried, I couldn't get my fingers to bleed; the calluses just kept getting thicker. Sometimes I would take my classical guitar with me to the cafeteria and play it while I waited in line. One day, a girl flipped my case open and tossed a dime in it. I said, "Wow! Thanks! That's the first actual money I've made playing my guitar!" She laughed. Then I said, "But am I really only worth a dime?" She giggled and went to the end of the line.

One of the most exciting things we did as a band was to play a few warehouse gigs in Tempe. We knew a guy whose father owned a warehouse, and he let us use it for a few shows. We bought a bunch of beer and posted fliers everywhere. It turned into quite the party, and we were the only band playing, which was exciting as could be. We made our own stage lights out of some PVC tubing that we "found" and some regular old lights. I guess that if you were stoned or drunk enough, the stage probably looked pretty cool!

One time we were invited to a "punker party." There was a group of hardcore punkers, with massive Mohawks and the works, who were almost like a gang, but they were totally cool. A friend told us about a party they were having and said I should bring my guitar, just in case, so I took it along. It was a good thing, too, because they wanted me to bring it in and play for them. It wasn't a tough crowd, by any means. Everyone was trashed drunk, as was I, so I'm sure I didn't sound that great. But I did have my Boss Digital Delay with me, and that was what made that night a memorable one. I made some of the most bizarre sounds with that and my guitar, and they just ate it up. It made me feel great, and we all left each other's' company in good spirits.

Many more parties like that ensued, and many more gigs, but the band fell apart at the end of the school year, and I moved up to Flagstaff with one of my best friends from high school, Tim.

In retrospect, I'm glad I got the time in on guitar; it really improved my abilities, and the experiences I had at ASU were life-changing ones that I will never forget. Not only that, during the past twenty-three years I have invested incredible amounts of time teaching myself, learning how to really play guitar, and learning how to read and write music. This has become an invaluable investment in me, and I have been reaping the rewards of it by teaching others and also by being sought after by professional bands for my talent. I fought long and hard for that talent. I have spent thousands and thousands of hours practicing, and I am proud of every moment. The people I have met through music have ranged from incredibly inept to totally incredible. I have experienced things that many people only read about, or dream about, and for that I will always be grateful.

The Healing Nature of Art

One of the main saving graces in my life has been art. Throughout my life, even before my interest in music, art has given me the strength to express the innermost pain and pleasures of life without having to tell someone else exactly what is going on within me. It has given me the gift of making others laugh through comical drawings, the ability to draw caricatures of others, and the opportunity for me to release, at least in some small way, some of the pressure created by repressing my feelings.

Art was important for me from the very beginning of my life. Dad is an artist, and our homes have always been filled with great and beautiful artwork: oil paintings, drawings, sculptures, and murals; you name it, it was in our home. While much of it was work that Dad created, a lot was the original work of other artists such as Bob Thompson, who is now a well-known painter, and whose paintings are much sought after. We had two of his Matisse-like  paintings in our house for as long as I can remember.

When I was little, Dad taught me how to draw a magician face in a top hat, using only a few lines and circles. He taught me a lot about photography, too, since he was a professor of photography at Drexel University, where he also taught drawing and painting.

Before my interest in music blossomed, I would spend hours and hours alone in my room, just drawing. At first it wasn't a conscious realization that drawing could help me feel better; rather,

I learned that from experiencing it. When I hit my teens and puberty, drawing became a helpful tool in releasing my inner frustration. I could draw myself, my true self, and bring who I really wanted to be out into the real world. And what was exciting about that was that I could show myself to others, and they didn't even know it was me that I had drawn. I spent many hours drawing the female figure, my female figure. Those drawings proved to be extremely therapeutic, and I don't think I would be where I am today without them, or without the ability to release my feelings in that way. It was amazing how that simple act had such an incredible power of release. But those were not the drawings I hung up on my walls. I was afraid they would make it obvious what I was struggling with. Those drawings were so close to me, so close to how I saw myself, that I feared anyone who saw them would see right through me to what I had been so afraid to acknowledge myself.

My next favorite thing to draw was cars, especially cartoonish ones. Cars represented freedom and independence, a way to get away from life as it was, and a way to be the person I really was, or really wanted to be. They were fun, and easy to draw, so I drew a lot of them. I was very much inspired by a great magazine called *CARtoons*, and my style became very much like that style of drawing: cartoons of cars. *CARtoons* was a car comic that featured excellent illustrative cartoon work and funny stories. I loved it a lot; it always made me laugh. That, and *Mad Magazine*, helped teach me the value of drawings that elicit laughter. I drew a lot of silly stuff over the years to make myself laugh, and I inadvertently made others laugh in the process. Not only did I find myself laughing out loud on many occasions, but I discovered that I could draw caricatures of my friends in high school and make them laugh, too. There was a period of time, in my junior and senior years in high school, that I would draw pictures of my friends during class. I would usually use a ballpoint pen and notebook paper, and after getting most of the image done, I would start to laugh uncontrollably. Sometimes I'd laugh so hard my teacher would ask me what was so funny. You know how that is: when you're not supposed to laugh, you just want to laugh that much more. I just kept picking people with unique features and drawing them. What a blast! It's no wonder I barely graduated from high school.

This cute vampire is one I drew to help me get through a long, boring day at work. He started out as a doodle, but then he turned out to be a rather cute little guy, I thought. He shall henceforth be known as Boris Von Doodleschtein!

Eventually, I began painting with oils. One of the paintings I did was of me as a female form, standing in a field with a breeze blowing. There was lots of color and movement in the painting; it was one of my favorite personal works. Unfortunately, Cindy smashed it over a post in the same fit of rage that destroyed my guitar. I have some digital pictures of the painting, one of which is on my Web site.

There are so many good reasons to draw, to paint, or to otherwise create, not the least of which is to release inner feelings you can't otherwise deal with. I cannot recommend highly enough the value of creating art for personal reasons. Most people mistakenly assume they cannot draw or paint because when they try to, their drawings are not aesthetically pleasing to them. I must say that most of an artist's drawings are not pleasing to the artist! We are our own worst critics. Also, everyone can draw. It is just like learning to write. When you first started to write, you probably were not so good, right? Well, learning to draw is just like learning to write, or just like learning anything. It is a skill that can be taught and learned, just like any other skill. There is nothing special about drawing; the people who are good at it have been practicing it for years. They have spent countless hours doing it, and they have drawn hundreds and hundreds of very crappy drawings in the process! So if you use the excuse that you can't draw, please think again, because I say you can. And if you want to learn more about that, I highly recommend you read a fantastic book called *Drawing on the Right Side of the Brain*, by Betty Edwards. Her book not only helped to improve my drawing skills, it helped me to look at the world in completely new and unique ways. These views of life and my surroundings in turn helped me to look more introspectively at myself in much the same manner, with a whole new set of eyes and a new perspective. Doing so helped me to better see myself where I was at the time, and where I wanted to be. I'm not sure that was the point of her book, but it sure worked well for me in that regard!

Writing—Self-Expression and Release

Writing, poetry and creating song lyrics have helped me cope with my frustrations in so many ways. Combining words with music has been deeply fulfilling, as it has combined two things I love so much. Good songwriting can be challenging, and very rewarding. The power of a well-crafted song can be immeasurable, and the feeling of creating a good song and moving people with it is beyond my ability to explain. But the songwriting process is not an easy one. It takes a lot of dedication and time to create good songs, and personally, I always had a hard time with it because I never really liked the sound of my singing voice.

It was the voice emanating from my body, but it wasn't *my* voice.

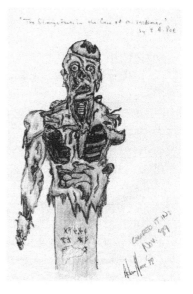

Writing stories became an integral part of my life when I was in high school. In fact, it was my English class, and more specifically my teacher, Mr. Bunger, who inspired me to write. It wasn't so much that he was a writer, but that he was really cool and an awesome teacher. One day during his class, I was drawing a picture of a corpse on top of a post with runes on it. The drawing was inspired by some horror movie I had seen and by my anatomy class, which was invaluable for learning how to draw body parts. It was pretty morbid. Since then, I have often wondered how much of a representation it was of how I had felt about my body at the time. As I was drawing it, Mr. Bunger walked by and saw it as he was passing out the graded homework. He said, "May I see that for a minute?" And I said, "Uh, I guess." And he took it to his desk. He wrote something on it and returned a minute later. As he slid it on my desk, I could see that on the top of the page he had written "'The Strange Facts in the Case of M. Valdemar' by E. A.

Poe."

Then he said, "This is really great. Nice work! It really reminds me of this story. You might enjoy it; it is pretty creepy!" I thanked him, but I didn't read the story until many years later. He had been right; it is a creepy story! I don't know what the runes I drew meant; I had made them up in the moment. Now, I think that this corpse represented me in many ways, and that the runes represented the mystery within me—that elusive "thing" I just could not pinpoint. There were times when I had wanted to tear my own skin off to reveal the real me underneath, although that was not something I actually had wanted to do, but the thought had given birth to some very vivid art and writing ideas.

Mr. Bunger had us write in journals every day, and we were required to turn them in for a grade. My friend, Tom, and I started writing some very strange, goofy stories just to fill in the pages, and that accelerated my learning how to write. One of my stories became somewhat of a local legacy; well, okay, it was mostly a legacy for Tom and me.

The story was called "A. S. S." It was about a young boy, Alfredo S. Suelo, who was completely indestructible. He wasn't a superhero; in fact, he was the opposite. He was basically a normal kid, but he had this incredible resilience to both pain and personal physical destruction. Thinking back on this now, I think he was a pretty good metaphor for me.

A. S. S. pulled out his teeth with vise grips; he jumped off skyscrapers, landed on the ground, and became a bloody pulp, only to gather his gooey parts back together, get up, get run over by a garbage truck, be dragged across town, and end up somewhere else for more destruction. The title was a link to how I felt: I felt like an ass because I felt so wrong in my own skin. There were times when I just wanted to peel away all the flesh from my bones to get down to what really mattered. Thinking back on that story, though, the one thing that really stands out to me now is the determination A. S. S. had. He never gave up. It was as if nothing in his control, not even his own incredibly creative efforts to do himself in, would erase the pain and agony that drove him. In the end, he couldn't change who he really was. It is almost as if I knew, even then, that I would never be able to change my self. Wow. That is pretty intense to look back on.

"A. S. S." became an ongoing saga in my English class journal, and several of my friends really enjoyed reading the regular episodes. Eventually, it became repetitive and boring, but I will never forget the very first line I wrote.

Once upon a time there was a boy named A. S. S. One day, A. S. S. decided to hit the road, so he walked outside, squatted down in the middle of the road, and punched it until his hand was a bloody stump.

Perhaps one day I'll put the saga on my Web site, or have it published, just for fun. I'm sure someone would probably get a kick out of it.

Writing has helped me in so many ways to overcome personal barriers. By writing out my feelings and thoughts, I am able to look at them more objectively, rather than being in the middle of my own pot of stew. In order to find satisfaction in our lives, we must overcome the barriers that keep us from being satisfied, but in order to do that we must first know what the barriers are. Do you know what you need in order to be truly satisfied? Do you need to be at peace within your own being? Do you need to completely change your body? Do you only need to change your behavior? Do you need the companionship of a lover or friend? Once you know what you need to make you happy, then you can start to figure out what the obstacles are that keep you from reaching your goal. Writing can help tremendously, and it doesn't take very much effort at all. Try this: Get a sheet of paper and a pen or pencil. At the top of the sheet, write your biggest goal, for example, "I want to own a house" (I'm going to keep this somewhat generic for now, so bear with me.) Underneath "House" make two columns. Label the column on the left "Obstacles to Come," and label the other one "Obstacles Overcome."

Now, in the "Obstacles to Come" column, make a list of all the things that you need to do or take care of in order to achieve your goal. In this case you might write, "Make more money," "Sell old car," "Apply for loan," "Pay off debt," and so on. These become sub-goals, or things you need to do in order to accomplish your big goal.

In the "Obstacles Overcome" column, write a list of all the sub-goals that you have already accomplished, or obstacles you have already overcome, that have brought you closer to the big goal of owning the house. These might be "Paid off debts," "Sold unneeded stuff," "Got better job," and so on.

As you write down sub-goals like "Make more money," you will notice that some items are just the tips of little icebergs; there is more to them than meets the eye. At first, this may appear overwhelming, but in reality it's probably nothing you don't already know about yourself or your situation. Often, the details, or the bottoms of the icebergs, are the things we really don't want to see, because they seem overwhelming. But they are far less overwhelming once you get them out of the dark and into the light— out of your subconscious and onto a piece of paper.

So, you've got your list(s) of sub-goals. Repeat the process and keep adding steps you need to take to achieve each sub-goal, until you get to where you are now. Some of these sub-goal lists may be one or two sub-goals deep, and other ones may be twenty deep. It just depends on the goal and how far you are from it. Once you get each sub-goal to the point where you can take the next step toward completing that sub-goal, then you can make a third list of all the "next steps" you need to take. Once you have this list of realistic things you can do to work toward your main goal, then you organize it into a priority order. After that…you start to really get things done.

All right, what are you still reading this for? Stick your bookmark in here now and go start your lists! Once you have them done, and you've prioritized your next steps, pick one and get to work on it! Then come back. I'll wait right here for you.

It really can be that simple to put things into perspective. It may seem basic, but it works great. I've been doing it for years, and without it I would be toast! Making lists like these helps get your perspective on your life a bit more clearly into view. Another thing that helps a lot is to have a nice little calendar, about 8.5 inches x 11 inches (print one out using your word processor; that's what I use) that you can write on and carry around with you if you need to. Calendars that clearly show each month so that you can easily write on the pages (in pencil!) are extremely valuable tools for organizing your life. I owe it to Cindy for getting me into this particular habit. Thank you, Cindy.

Okay, so while I'm on a "recommending spree" here, I have to recommend something else, especially to my trans sisters (not to be confused with transistors, capacitors, or potentiometers), and that is this: get a journal and start using it. Now! Don't be afraid that someone else might read it. If you are more concerned with what other people think, then you need a journal more than ever. If you haven't started a personal journal out of fear that someone, your wife, husband, lover, mother, father, or whoever, would find it, then just get one and find a safe spot to stash it. It's important. Besides, anyone worth his or her salt who finds your journal won't read it. Journals are a fantastic tool for releasing the vast array of feelings that can often cause torrents of anger, fear, depression, and all kinds of negative emotions, without putting yourself in a risky social situation with others. You can purge your psyche of those thoughts, feeling, and ideas by writing about them. Not only that, but often when you put your feelings down in black and white, you can get a clearer picture of what is driving you, what is motivating you. And having a clearer picture always helps you overcome things in your life that need to be overcome.

There's also another excellent benefit of journaling, and that is the "time machine" effect. After you have been keeping journals for a year or more, you can flip an old journal open to the page that is dated a year ago and see what you were doing and thinking about then. And hopefully, you can see just how far you've come along in your journey of life. I honestly believe that if it were not for the journals I've kept over the years, I would not have made it through all this. Please consider getting one, if you don't already keep one. They're cheap to buy and priceless in the end.

Part II:
Tuning Up

How Do You *Know*?

In struggling to ascertain just who we are and where we fall in the spectrum of gender, many questions arise: How do you really know if you're transsexual or exactly where you fall within the spectrum of gender? Is there even a particular spot we are supposed to fall into, or is it an ever-changing landscape of gender experience? When you grow up as a boy, but your head is seeing, feeling, thinking, and generally perceiving life as a girl, how do you even know what the word *gender* means? I don't think I ever even knew what gender was, or at least what it was like to be a gender. Being both genders simultaneously gives a person a distorted view of all that, at least at first. But once you learn that your gender identity and your body sex are essentially mismatched, this larger understanding of who you are, who you've been, and who you can possibly be starts to become much more clearly defined. That, however, can take up half a lifetime. And, of course, it can cause emotional stress not only for you, but for others in your immediate family.

Knowing yourself as soon as possible in life is perhaps one of the keys to an overall better outcome; however, there are so many things to take into account. If you got married, had children, and built a family, how do you know if you should risk losing everything you have in order to find true inner peace and happiness? How do you know whether, after risking it all, you would be any happier than you are right now? We are the only ones who can answer these questions for ourselves; often, even we can't answer them until we have evolved in our journey and come to a point where we can look back at what we have done in honest retrospect.

If you talk to a counselor or psychologist about your transgender feelings, that person will probably not make suggestions as to what you should do about your situation. It is not for a counselor or therapist, or anyone, to tell another person what choices to make in life; however, these professionals will help you figure out what you want to do about your situation. My goal, in lending my experience and thoughts to our community, is to help people figure out what they should do, given their particular circumstances and feelings, and to provide an example of how things might work out.

Most importantly, you have to weigh your options: How strong are your feelings? Do you wish you were female? Do you enjoy being male? Do you enjoy being each at different times? How long have you been dealing with these feelings? Ever since you can remember? Usually, people who feel the desire to be the opposite sex have the feelings and thoughts from their earliest memories. This is a common thread among those with the transsexual condition, and it makes perfect sense, considering we are born with it. If you lived alone on an island and could be whichever you wanted to be, which would you be? If you would be the opposite of what you are now, then why would you be the opposite on an island, but not in the place you currently live? What is keeping you from changing your life now? I think this is a good place for this reminder: We do not choose to be born into the transsexual condition. This is most certainly *not* a lifestyle! It is simply who we are.

Most of us who go through with full transitions and genital reconstructive surgery (GRS) follow an incredibly similar course through our lives. "Genital reconstructive surgery" seems to make more sense than "sexual reassignment surgery" because it is, after all, our genitals that are being reconstructed, not our sex that is being reassigned. By the time most of us have surgery, we are already most of the way through reassigning our sex anyway! Although those of us who go through with full transitions may be very different in terms of our careers or in where we live, there are amazing similarities in our lives: repression, depression, wondering in the beginning if we're just cross-dressers, trying to convince ourselves that what we're feeling isn't real, attempting transition and going back to the old us, but then eventually completing full transitions. If we have established our lives as males with families, children, and masculine careers in attempts to mask our real feelings, then we make it that much harder to open ourselves up to finding peace and tranquility in our lives. We box ourselves in with so much that we make it almost impossible to get out.

Have you boxed yourself in with a masculine life? Do you feel trapped, not only in your own flesh, but in your entire existence?

Do you tell yourself that you shouldn't transition because you don't think you'll pass? Hey, I felt that way, too. Sometimes I still do. But I've discovered that feelings around the idea of passing are based on the social gender dichotomy. The world is comfy in the assumption that there are only two sexes. Not only that, but natal women (women born female, also referred to as "gg's" in the transgender community, which is short for "genetic girls") can feel just as strongly about passing, or looking good in public as transsexual women. Our society places such high value on the way we look. So even without gender-related issues, people feel strong desires to fit in and be accepted. The extreme definition of male and female roles slams us all into behavior patterns that are not necessarily natural, but rather created by humans in large measure for the purpose of manipulating others and for selling products to consumers. Just turn on your television and take a look at how this divisive dichotomy controls us.

Think about groups, individuals, religions, governments, companies, news channels, and others promote extremes of the gender/sex dichotomy, and how they actively campaign against the rights of the LGBT community. This affects not only our community, but the whole of our society. Think about how you and the way you live your life have been affected.

How can we change the lack of a real appreciation and acceptance of differences of LGBT people? How can we end the campaign against the rights of the LGBT community? How can we fix it so that people don't feel oppressed for not fitting into the boxes? Is it even something that we could completely change, even if we wanted to? I believe this is something that needs to be changed, or adjusted, in order for all people to feel comfortable in the world, and in their own skins. The more people there are in the world, the more dramatic the problem could become. We need relief, we need resolution, and we need acceptance and equality on a global scale. It is a battle for freedom of individuality, and we fight not only for our own personal freedom, but for the freedom of the many others like us. We stand not just for our own rights, but for the rights of all who are different, all who feel oppressed, all who hold themselves back from realizing a full and happy life, all who have the same rights as anyone else on this earth.

There are things we can say we know for sure, and there are things we can say we think we know, or believe, but about which we are not absolutely sure. The transsexual condition seems to be one of those things that falls in the latter category, at least until we reach the threshold of self-acceptance. That threshold is essentially the point at which we realize that this thing, this feeling in our heads, whatever it may be, is not going to leave us alone or go away. Sometimes it takes years, if not decades, for us to finally admit this to ourselves. I am sure there must be some people who never do admit it, and they try to cope with it until they depart this world, but it can never go away because it simply is part of who we are.

Thankfully, most of us do finally accept the fact that there is, indeed, something "wrong" with us. As more time passes, and as I meet and talk with more and more transsexuals, the more I realize that we, as individuals, are not what is wrong with this picture. It is not that we are "broken" people or that we are blemished goods from the assembly line of life. We are who we are, whether we are this way because of an anomaly of genetics, chance, biology, or the hand of God. The simple fact is this: we are born with the transsexual condition. And there are many of us. So many, in fact, that we can no longer consider ourselves "wrong," or anomalies. We are not errors of production; we are unique and rare, and we are meant to be.

Someone once said that we are freaks or wrong; that we are mistakes. We do not choose to be born, and surely we do not choose to be born differently from everyone else, not when it means so much judgment and oppression. If we were able to know what the consequences of our birth would be, would we choose instead to stay unborn and never live our lives? What is most astonishing is that all people are nearly identical in terms of genetic makeup, yet we are all incredibly unique. Why is it that some believe that the way they are is right, and that others are wrong and should be like them? Who do they think they are to make such judgments upon others, human beings who are every bit as equal, and who have every bit as much right to be and express themselves in this world that we all share? We cannot continue to let others oppress us. They will not stop unless we stop them by standing up for our essential human rights. We must be proactive, and if we are not, then perhaps they are right after all.

As we move forward into the future of humankind, there are many questions we all face. We live in a world of terror and war. We are in a massive shift in global social and economic relations, and yet here we are, all of us, each of us, dealing with our own personal issues, struggling to be who we are.

I have thought about what I see in the picture of humanity to come. At times I have been frightened by thoughts of nuclear holocaust, of continents falling into the oceans, of asteroids crashing into our world. I have imagined overpopulation and the ensuing problems that would come from that. I have thought about my son being here years after I am gone, and what the world might be like then. What will the world be like for his children? Will it be a happy place to live, to thrive? Or will it be filled with hatred and prejudice, war and tyranny? Will the children of my son's children find peace in their lives? Will they be free to be themselves, no matter who they are or how they appear? Will they ask their parents about their great-grandmother who changed her sex, or will that just not matter anymore by then?

As I make my way, moment by moment, through this life, I think about what I wish the world to be like for those who follow in my footsteps—my son, other transsexuals, others who are regarded as outcasts because of who they are—and I see a picture of freedom. I see a picture of compassion, education, and understanding. I see a world full of men, women, and children with open minds and open hearts—unafraid of people who are unique or different, unafraid of their own uniqueness or differences. I imagine a world that does not attempt to box its people into the two boxes of the current bigender idiom. This is a world where there is true freedom of self-expression, without fear of reprisals from ignorant people who do not even know us.

This is the world for which I strive. These are the people for whom I work.

I don't think I will ever understand the technical or biological reasons that I'm transsexual...and I am transsexual. I have struggled very hard for the better part of at least twenty years to try to understand this mystery, but it's like trying to understand why life itself exists. There is no explanation that we could hope to understand, so we must surrender to the unknown and accept the fact that there is no reason, other than it just exists.

It's a bit like trying to understand exactly what love is, or feels like, or what the Grand Canyon is like if you've never been there before. There's really no way to describe it with words. That's because words are conscious and tangible elements. Dealing with transsexualism comes from a much deeper, less tangible, less objective place than that, and it is not, in itself, a conscious thing. It is not a decision we make, as many people assume. However, we must ultimately make a conscious decision about what to do about being this way, but we most certainly do not wake up one day and say, "Hey! I'm gonna risk it all and change my sex!" It is there from day one. Those who think that we just up and decided to change our sex one day simply have no understanding about this subject. Without some understanding, there can be no compassion. Without compassion there can be no acceptance. They have never seen it from our perspective, but with a bit of understanding, very good things could happen.

Lack of understanding engenders fear, and fear brings out all kinds of negative energy that causes people not only to say, but also to do, hurtful and terrible things. As a misunderstood group in society, we fear those reactions from others, so we hide from them in our own fear. We repress our feelings. We suppress what we know. We hide the truth of who we really are. We hide ourselves from ourselves. We become good at covering up. Our conscious mind, driven by our subconscious mind's barrages of fear, guilt, shame, and anger, makes us do things that would prove to ourselves, prove to the world, that we are nothing less than the men we're "supposed to be."

Many of us create a strong psychological wall that defends us from the outside world's discovery of our embarrassing secret. The strength of that wall is built from bricks of fear, held together by a mortar of confusion and an incredible amount of feeling like we are the only one in the world with such a conundrum. We do the most masculine things we can, in a futile attempt to prove to ourselves and the world that there's not something completely and utterly wrong with us. We become everything we think a man is supposed to be to prove this to ourselves: We join the armed forces. We find girlfriends. We get married. We become fathers. All because we think we can prove ourselves wrong, or that it's "just a phase," or as a futile attempt to fix ourselves.

Most of us, after years, decades even, finally come to grips with our nature and admit we're fighting a losing battle against ourselves and accept ourselves for how we truly are. Some of us decide that it's just too much to bear, and take the express checkout lane of life to try to make the pain go away. But luckily, and often with the love, help, and compassion of others, most of us finally realize that we have a problem that needs to be addressed. Then we begin the often painful and arduous journey of letting go of our fears, shames, and guilt to release ourselves and to be free to be who we really are. Unfortunately, it is all too common that we also lose most of our family members and friends. But then there are those who don't. I am lucky enough to say that I am one who has not lost my family and I have only lost a few friends, and I am thankful and proud of them for being there for me.

Adding Value—To Yourself

A common business concept is the "value add"—adding value to the product or job that a company offers its customers. Something I think that far too often we fail to add value for is ourselves. Until after I gave myself permission to just be myself, and transitioned from who I wasn't to who I am, I didn't realize just how little value I was giving myself. I did not have a very positive sense of self-worth; in fact, I would say my level of self-worth was at nearly zero most of the time. Looking back, I can see why, obviously. When you're in the throes of dealing with something so monumental, so life affecting, something you believe you can't deal with, let alone understand, and something you try to hide from everyone, even yourself, it tends to demolish your self-worth.

Without self-worth, it is almost impossible to give much of yourself to the rest of the world, or to family, friends, and work. When I was caught in the toughest moments of repression, frustration, and denial, I would pour myself into my work—music, working on things, fixing stuff, making things, playing sports, whatever, so that I didn't have to think about it—so that I could avoid myself. Well, because you are yourself, you can't be avoided by yourself. Although, when you're in the midst of that fray, avoidance sure seems like the best way to deal with the situation. But now that I've come out the other side, I have to say that I no longer think that it is the right way to deal with it. Avoiding the issues and avoiding yourself has a tendency to remove value from one's self, until what is left? An empty, sad, and miserable person? Perhaps.

There must be a way that we can add value to ourselves. But we cannot do so when we are struggling to keep such major parts of ourselves hidden. The only way to increase our sense of self-worth is to deal with those issues head on, to open our eyes, all three of them, and see ourselves for who, or what, we really are. We need to honestly accept ourselves, and all the big and small things that make us different from the norm, so that we can clear our heads, hearts, and souls, and clear away the noise that keeps us from allowing ourselves to exist completely.

The only way to add value to one's self is to like yourself. If you do not like who you are, then you will have little positive in your life. It is scary when you face the thought, "I'm a boy on the outside, but I'm a girl on the inside!" because that is not something that we hear about very often, and when we do, it is something that is often ridiculed or used as the butt of a joke. How can people like themselves when the world around them says they are worthless? Even if the world does not directly tell you that you're worthless because you are different, you still feel that way by proxy. It is a sad, depressing way to live, and very challenging to change.

Once you work through the issues and step into the new realm of yourself, as you let go of the negative feelings—self-hatred, low self-esteem—you find that these dark feelings have been replaced with something new: space! The mental energy required to repress one's transsexual condition is immense. Using your energy to repress can become dark and foreboding, and it can literally consume your ability to interact successfully with the world. When you take care of yourself—when you get therapy, go to support groups, realize you're not alone, know that you really can do something about it, and allow yourself the freedom to be who you are—then you find that all the negative mental (and spiritual) energy you had been using is now available for other things. Not only that, but there is no more distraction. No more hidden weight on your shoulders. No more voice in the back of your head saying, "Something is wrong. You're a girl, dammit! What are you doing? What are you waiting for?" And those new reserves of energy burst forth!

You can then use that energy, that now positive energy, for so many things, most of which will be positive just by the very nature of the circumstances. There is so much more clarity; life becomes crystal clear.

There are still challenges to be faced, though, and just because one accepts one's particular plight and goes through the transition process does not mean that life will be perfect. It's life, and with life comes so many challenges. But what is amazing is that one is so much more ready to take on challenges; after overcoming the challenges of transsexualism, the rest seem like nothing at all, especially if you are happy.

It is all about feeling good about yourself. If you don't, then whether you make it obvious to the world or not, the world will pick up the energy you give off. I believe this is true, because when I finally overcame my issues, my transsexual condition, and gained back all that wasted energy, I found myself feeling incredible! In my day-to-day living the comfort and happiness I feel within emanates from me in my smiles and laughs, in the positive sound of my voice, and the positive way I treat others. Some people tell me I have a quiet calm and very centered quality—that I seem very much at peace with myself. This is very true! I believe that this energy affects not only the way others perceive me, but how they relate to me and how they treat me in return. That affects how much they want to be near me. When people want to be near you, you gain a lot of positive control and power. Power that can be used for achieving your dreams and goals.

As great as it sounds to just accept ourselves for who we are and jump right into changing our lives, it is not that simple, of course. If it were, we wouldn't be struggling to deal with the situation. So in an effort to manage the feelings, we end up doing a lot of things that occupy our mental time so we don't have to think about our situation as much. In doing so, we tend to get really good at certain things. Most of the time, these things are just methods of escape, but interestingly, whatever it is we end up doing often ends up being one way of adding value to ourselves, although we didn't think of it that way.

For me, I plunged into art—writing, drawing, music, and computers. Sometimes I wonder how much better my art and music would be if I had never had all that frustration, confusion, and repression sucking away copious amounts of my creative energy for all those years. But then I have to wonder if I would be half the artist I am now if I hadn't gone through all that I did. Personal struggle and tragedy sometimes seem to have a way of bringing out the best in us. Perhaps that is because we are reminded just how much we really want something, or how much we really don't want something. Or maybe it is that we just don't give a damn, so risk becomes something we don't care about at all. And life without risk, well, that's no life at all. Either way, one can turn the energy to positive or negative outcomes; however, it really is best to clear away or fix that which is causing the problems. When we are in excellent condition—mentally, physically, emotionally, spiritually—and when we are running smoothly, like a well-oiled machine, life becomes much better. But sometimes it just takes us a long time to figure that out, or to realize that something is actually wrong. So in that case, it is good that we have something positive to turn to for release of pent up frustrations. And for me, art was it.

Let's Get One Thing "Straight"

Before transition, one of the things I often heard from people when I told them about myself was that they thought I must be gay. One of the first questions they asked was, "Does this mean you're gay?" A friend of mine asked if I visited gay bars to look for dates. I was quite perturbed by his assumption and tried to explain to him the facts about myself and my sexuality. For whatever reasons, or misconceptions, he assumed that because my body was originally male, and that I liked men, that I must be gay. People don't take into account gender identity as being something separate from body sex. With regard to sexuality, most people think only in terms of body sex and sexual preference. Interestingly, the labels gay, straight, bi and lesbian are determined more by gender identity and sexual preference, and have little or nothing to do with body sex! This may sound strange at first, but let me explain further.

The definition of gay or straight becomes rather vague when applied to those dealing with transsexualism, given the circumstances, and there is no blame to be given to those who don't understand this yet; they are just naive and need the proper education. Hopefully what follows will help remove these particular misconceptions about transsexuals, and about LGBT people in general, once and for all.

There are three essential elements to a person's sexuality. Most of us hardly even give a moment's thought to this idea, let alone realize that there are three distinctly different aspects at play for each of us:

- *Body sex*—the physical sex of your flesh, your body; male or female. Body sex is determined primarily by chromosomes, which dictate the physical sexual development of the fetus, then secondarily, by the hormones produced by the reproductive organs.
- *Gender Identity*—a person's "mental sex," or the mental image of one's physical sex. This is a complex and somewhat obscure concept, and most people do not even realize its existence. The majority of people have a gender identity that is congruent with their body sex, so they never even think about the fact that there are

actually two separate aspects involved. A person's gender identity is usually either male or female, although I have known some rare folks out there who differ from this. There are some who straddle the line and enjoy spending time as one or the other, depending on their mood or the situation.

- *Sexual Preference*—who gets us sexually aroused: men, women, both, or neither. "Both" means that they are "bisexual." "Neither" is generally described as "non-sexual." But the other two are where the lines of definition can become blurred.

Body Sex	Gender Identity	Sexual Preference	Type or Label
Male	Male	Female	Straight
Male	Male	Male	Gay
Female	Female	Male	Straight
Female	Female	Female	Lesbian
Male	Female	Male	Straight, transsexual
Male	Female	Female	Lesbian, transsexual
Female	Male	Female	Straight, transsexual
Female	Male	Male	Gay, transsexual

To make this a bit easier to comprehend, think of it as a mathematical formula:

Gender Identity + Sexual Preference = Gay, Straight, Bi, and so on. Body sex is essentially not part of the equation.

This makes it more apparent that the labels "gay" or "straight" are not based on body sex, but rather on gender identity and sexual preference. Our gender identity is what we perceive our body sex to be. Take me, for example. I was born with male body parts; my body sex was male. However, because of variables in my fetal development, my brain did not develop as male along with my body and has remained essentially female. There are numerous scientific reports about how this happens, which are available from many sources, one of the most detailed of which can be found in the online journal *The International Journal of Transgenderism*. To simply state it, though, when the human fetus develops, it begins as female. All humans start development as females, and then, when chromosomes dictate that the developing fetus is to become male, certain changes begin to take place. There are a number of events during gestation called "hormonal washes," in which the male fetus to be is exposed to high levels of testosterone. These washes trigger biological development in the brain and reproductive organs of the fetus. Sometimes for developing males, however, these washes are incomplete, or nonexistent, and do not provide a high enough level of testosterone to trigger changes the fetuses' brains needs to develop in the male direction. This is the best I can describe it in brief for you. I encourage you to learn more about it online or in your local library. Learning about this concept has helped me tremendously in understanding the transsexual condition.

Because my brain has always seen me as female, I essentially have always been a girl; it's just that it wasn't evident on the outside. This helps to explain why, throughout the ages, trans women have said they were "women trapped in men's bodies," for it is literally true. Being this way is very confusing, let me assure you, because you have part of your psyche telling you that you're female, while you have a very obvious body part telling you that you are male. Which do you think you would listen to more? The thing dangling between your legs, I'm sure! At first, it is very hard for us to understand, or accept, that we are transsexual, very hard. It is much easier to assume that we're crazy, or going through a phase, or that this thing will pass if we just act more manly or repress it more. Sometimes it takes a lifetime to accept it. And it does not go away! We cannot judge a person's gender identity by their skin or body sex. And only they can tell us what their gender identity is.

So, in my case, I was male, and my gender identity is female, and I am sexually attracted to men. This makes me heterosexual. Body sex has nothing to do with it. I am not gay, because I do not want sex as a man, with a man. I am straight because I want sex as a woman, with a man. If I were gay, then I would have enjoyed having a penis, being a man, and sharing my male body with another man. But I am not, and never have been, a man, and I now have totally female anatomy, without a uterus and ovaries, and therefore

I will be a woman with a man.

I used to tell people when they would ask me if I were gay, "No. If I were gay, I'd actually want this penis, want to be a man, and would enjoy sharing my manly self with other men. However, I am a woman, who wants to be the woman I am, with a man." Sometimes it takes a while to grasp it, but it seems to sink in eventually. Often, people have naïvely stated that they think we change our sex because we're afraid to admit that we're gay. This statement is a pathetic attempt to make themselves feel better about their ignorance by demeaning us. It is also a reminder that with age, maturity does not always follow.

Interestingly, it is usually men who asked me, "Does this mean you're gay?" The vast majority of women I have told do not relate the news to something of a sexual sort. For some reason they seem more apt to understand that it has more to do with who I am than who I want to have sex with. I find this especially interesting, and I think it may indicate higher levels of homophobia in men than in women. Maybe it has something to do with me having been male and then changing my sex; perhaps the realization that it is possible strikes a chord in them...I don't know. I may never know. But it is quite interesting to observe.

Then there is the assumption that trans women "used to be men." We were never men. It is so easy to assume that because a person had a male body for thirty years that this person was a man, but it's not true. How much of a person is their flesh? And how much of them is who they are inside, their personality, their experience, feelings and beliefs? As human beings, we are the sum result of our personalities, our character, our memories, and the experiences we've had throughout our lives. The things we learn and understand, and the pain and pleasure we experience, are all factors that make up who we are. Genes and fetal development also make us who we are, as does the physiology of the most complex structure we know of, our brain. If you are not transsexual in any way, then perhaps you are lucky, because you know what it is like to experience simply being male or female. I do not know what that is like. Since I have never been completely male, and I will never be completely female, I will never know what it is like to be one or the other.

But maybe I'm one of the lucky ones...because even though

I do not know what it is like to be either male or female, I do know what it is like to be both male and female. I can't tell you what it means to be a man. I wasn't one. I was a girl with a boy's skin, and then a girl with a man's skin. All the while I felt very lost, alone, and incredibly isolated from the world, from my friends, and from my family, and even from myself. Although I don't know what it was like to actually be a boy or a man, I do know what it was like to have the experiences of a boy and a man, because I did experience many things from a male perspective. You might now be more able to understand just how confusing and frustrating it was to have to experience those things, given that I was really a girl the whole time.

Now that I have had GRS, I know far more what it feels like to be female because I am now closer than I've ever been to that person who I have always felt I am. I actually feel normal for the first time in my life. Talk about a weight lifted, a burden removed, a stone off the shoulders. All I can say is that it sure does feel damn good to finally be free of the incongruence of gender dysphoria. That stuff is a bitch!

This all leads to a question you may be thinking now, one that I have asked myself many times throughout my life: "So with all this, why have I spent my sexual life primarily with other women. Doesn't that make me a lesbian? What the hell?" The answer has been elusive, but recently I came to some realizations. I could not be with men because I was externally male. That idea made me feel uncomfortable because the thought of two males being sexually active together doesn't do it for me; it just does not turn me on. Two women together don't bother me, although it is not my preference. But the thought of being female with a male has always turned me on, and it has always seemed very natural and normal to me. This was extremely confusing when I was a teenager, to say the least. I had what I considered then to be strange fantasies about being a girl with a guy. That has always been my sexual desire, and you can imagine how impossible it was to fulfill my desires. It took me a long time to realize that what I was having were not abnormal sexual thoughts after all; I just did not know who I was at the time, or what was going on with me.

The best recourse I had, once I became sexually active, was to be with girls, because then I was closer to what I didn't have. The most important part of that was the fact that I could live vicariously through sex—in my mind I became the other woman, the one I was with. That was the best way I could cope with my incongruence in terms of sexual satisfaction, aside from masturbation, which was also a good alternative for getting through my sexual frustration, even thought it was never truly fulfilling.

On a few occasions, even before I began to think about transition, I did have sex with two different guys. Those times were when I was still outwardly male and before I had made the decision to change. I had a very good time with one of them in particular, and he with me, even though he didn't know that I was transsexual. After having had vicarious sex for so many years already, it was pretty easy to use the same mental techniques with him. Ultimately, though, it was very frustrating and unfulfilling, and it still felt wrong to me because my body was wrong. I needed more…I needed to be me. But it would still be many years before I would attempt to fix my situation.

Little Girl Lost. Woman Missing.

For years I thought I was crazy. Even as I would think those thoughts though, I would know that I really wasn't losing my mind. As a matter of fact, I always thought that my mind was the one thing I actually did have! I started to research some things I had heard about from somewhere. I don't even remember where I first heard about them: transvestism, homosexuality, fetishes. They were all names of things I didn't understand and had no idea if they fit me.

I researched all the new concepts about identity and gender that I had heard about on television or from peers or others, but none of them seemed to fit me. I was intrinsically different. My sense of being different was more closely tied to my body and to who I was in terms of gender and body sex. While it had something to do with clothes, they were just tools to help me get closer to who I was; what I wore was not the cornerstone of my issue.

Then one day at the library, I found some information about transsexualism. Once I read it, I knew I had found my answer, even though I couldn't understand why it was the way it was. Although I could finally put a label on my problem, it was another matter altogether to try to accept it as the truth and as my reality. I had been so good at repressing my feelings that it took me a few years to accept the fact that I was, indeed, living with the transsexual condition. A few years later, when I was in my mid-thirties, I finally found some scientific research data that said transsexuals, those who feel like "women trapped in men's bodies," really do have female brains because of certain fetal developmental anomalies. To clearly understand that this was how I was, a female brain in a male body, completely opened my eyes to the truth, and from then on, I started seeking answers to dealing with my problem. It was, however, not a singular problem…it was simply the can with all the worms in it, and I had just taken off the lid.

Stepping into a new way of being wasn't easy, considering my life: family, friends, and job. I didn't want to lose all that; I didn't want anything else to change, just my sex. But how can someone change his or her sex and expect everything else to just stay the same way it was? It can't be. Too many things change for everything else to stay the same. Changing sex is an intrinsic change that affects almost everything we are, yet we are still essentially the same person we have always been. That doesn't necessarily mean that the changes are bad. Even though there is the potential for great loss, in terms of family, friends, jobs, and basic rights and freedoms (not to mention all the ways in which women in general are treated), the changes can be incredibly positive ones in terms of happiness…true happiness.

One of the most profound questions I have strived to answer for myself during the past six or seven years is this: "If I have always been sexually attracted to men, why have I always been with a woman?" This has been the most perplexing thing for me, because since 1985 I had deeply loved Cindy and no one else. Prior to my transition, my experiences with both men and women were not fully satisfying, and there was a deep conflict for me during them because my body wasn't female. Even with the frustration that came from them, the encounters were good and bad, for different reasons.

In order to uncover an answer to my question, I thought it was important to go back to my teens and to the highly repressive state I was in at the time. When I was a teenager, I found myself intensely attracted to girls, but for a number of different reasons that I think had little relationship to the reasons my male friends were attracted to them. They were attracted to them on almost purely sexual levels and often spoke of wanting to have sex with girls they found attractive. "Damn, she's hot! I'd love to get with her!" they would say, and they would, of course, be far more graphic about how they wanted to "get" with a girl. My reaction was a half-smile, or a quick voicing of approval, but inside I was thinking, "Oh my God, I would love to have a body like hers!" It's important to emphasize that my male friends were just that, friends. I was not sexually attracted to them at all.

As I experienced the fiery passions of youth within me, my own passions ignited a wide variety of perplexing feelings and thoughts. While my body became physically aroused at the site of a beautiful girl, it was not specifically because I was sexually attracted to her, but more so that I was attracted to what she represented: what I felt in myself. I knew that if I looked like she did, not only would I feel "normal," but also my sexual fantasies and desires might likely be attained. Interestingly, the girls I was attracted to were girls I most looked like, or girls I thought would look like me if I were female. In an intriguing chain of mental events, I would instantly become myself, the girl I saw in my head, and I could then be free to be myself in gender and sexual terms. It became a vicarious way of living, and while helpful in many ways, it was not without its drawbacks.

The main drawback of mentally becoming the girl I saw in my head was that it was utterly confusing for me at the time. I had no idea what was going on in my head, and I had nothing objective to compare it to. I could not empathize with my male friends about sex or sexuality at all. The only time I felt I could relate to someone else about sex was when I was dating girls. Interestingly, when I dated, it was not about having sex; rather, it was quite the opposite. It was more about learning what it was like to be female. I recall dozens of dates with girls when we just sat and talked about all kinds of things, "girl things," and I guess none of them ever wondered why I was interested in such topics. One night, when I dropped a friend off at her house, I said good night, and she said, "Wow, that's really amazing."

I said, "What is?"

She said, "That you didn't even try anything with me. You didn't try to make out with me." She would probably understand it better if she knew me now.

This isn't to say that I didn't have sex with girls—I did. When I look back at why, I find that there were two main reasons: first of all, it was the closest I could get to being female. I mean, if I couldn't be female, then I could at least get as close as possible to the female body I wanted. While this was relief in some ways, it also compounded my frustration in many other ways. The second reason was vicarious sex. From the very first time I had sex with a girl, in the back of my station wagon, until the last time, I experienced it vicariously as a woman at the same time as I was experiencing it in a man's skin. I imagined I were her and that she were me, and whatever I did for her is what I thought I would like. From what I recall, this worked out really well for my partners, but it made life very frustrating for me. I could not yet fully understand why I behaved that way. More and more I felt like I was unable to be myself, unable to live my own life. I was also living a lie in another way. I wasn't being able to literally express who I was, but even more importantly, I wasn't able to experience who I was. It was good enough at the time, and with repression of those feelings I was somehow able to cope, but it was more air into the balloon: eventually, I was going to run out of space.

After I left Arizona State, I moved north to Flagstaff, where one of my best friends from high school, Tim, had been living. He had a small apartment and was kind enough to let me stay with him until I got on my feet. He even came down to Tempe to help me move. Tim and I had had many great times together: we went to US Fest '83, and we made it to many excellent heavy metal shows in Phoenix. To this day, he remains one of my best friends. Tim was always there for me when I was down and needed a friend, and in many ways, I was there for him, too. I guess that's what being friends is all about, isn't it?

It was in Flagstaff that Cindy and I met. The second day after moving there, I asked Tim what there was to do for fun in Flag, and if there were any good video game arcades. He said, "Yeah, at the mall." So we went to the mall to scope out the video game scene. We parked and walked into the mall through the main entrance. Down the corridor, which had no shops but was just one of those little mall  courtyards that lead into the main mall area, we could see two girls sitting on a low wall. One was a bleached blond, and the other was a stunning redhead. The closer we got to them, and the closer I got to her, the more my heart began to race. There was something incredible about this girl; I could feel it. There was electricity in the air, an excitement that was undeniable. Our eyes met, our souls touched, and I fell in love with her instantly. As Tim and I walked past them, it was hard for me not to stare at her. I suggested that we duck into the B. Dalton Bookseller store immediately to our right because they had started following us. Coincidentally, it was the same store where Cindy's mom worked.

"I think they're following us!" I said, grabbing a *Hit Parader* magazine and pretending to read it. Tim agreed, and a moment later the two girls walked past the store, looking in there for us and giggling when they saw us. They kept walking. We followed in hot pursuit. Loudly, so we would be sure to hear, Cindy said, "Yeah, let's go to the library!" And they headed out of the mall. We ran to my car. We raced around the parking lot, found them, and followed them to a nearby fast food drive-thru. Some funky library they have in Flagstaff! Somehow I managed to give Cindy our address, and the next morning as I was still waking up from the haze of sleep, the two girls knocked on our door. I invited them in, and we shared some scrambled eggs. The rest, as they say, is history.

Cindy was beautiful, smart, and funny. And on top of it all, she was just like me—our attitudes and tastes in music and things in general were almost identical. It wasn't just because we were so much alike that I was attracted to her, though. She was funny and extremely smart, and she liked me, really liked me a lot. For the first time in my life, I felt like I had finally found someone I could relate to, someone who could relate to me. On so many levels we were the perfect match, and I will even take a chance and say that I think we still are and always will be. There was a magic between us; it was like a drug to us both. She was everything I wanted to be and everything I wanted from a partner. I essentially had decided that it wasn't possible for me to be a girl, because I obviously was not one then, so I had relinquished myself to what my body dictated. I loved her with intense passion. Our minds and personalities fit together like puzzle pieces, and our bodies fit together perfectly, too. I fell deeply in love with her, and she with me, and for most of our lives we remained absolutely inseparable, until I could no longer maintain the mental energy required to suppress my true self.

We spent a few years together before we considered marriage. Ironically, or perhaps not, it was she who proposed the idea. "Well, we're going to be together forever anyway." We agreed, "It's just a technicality." And so we decided to do it. I really did believe we would be together forever, for better or worse, 'til death we do part. In a strange way, I guess we were together until a kind of death parted us, for Cindy did marry Adam, and Adam did die in a way. I know, it's not just the outside of us that we marry; it is the whole package. But when a woman loves a man, and she marries a man, she wants to be with a man. Life can be tough and confusing sometimes, but perhaps ours is not to question why so much as it is just to experience the gift of life and the gifts that it brings us—the people who love us.

Our wedding was beautiful. Cindy looked stunningly gorgeous in her dress. I have to admit I was very jealous! I wore a tuxedo, with tails, and while I should have tied my hair back, I just left it down, somewhat un-styled. She thought I looked handsome, and I got many nice compliments, but I didn't feel handsome at all; I just felt out of place. Not out of place with her or with our families, but out of place with myself. When you feel out of sorts within your own being, it really is hard to feel as though you fit in to anything at all.

It was a small ceremony, with our immediate families and a few others from Cindy's extended family. It took place in the backyard of Cindy's grandparents' house. The yard was beautifully decorated. Our song was "Thank You" by Led Zeppelin. I still cry when I hear it, because it brings back those memories and those strong feelings of love and commitment we had. Sometimes my heart feels clenched into a knot then; it just hurts. The vows I made, and the commitment I made to her, I meant it—every word of it— and I find that even now I still love her so incredibly much, for worse, for better, until I die…my love for her seems only to have increased over the years.

Perhaps it was a symbol of things to come, or perhaps just another random occurrence, but on the way back to our home in Phoenix, our car broke down in the middle of the desert several miles outside of Gila Bend. To our amazement, a tow truck happened to be driving the other way not long after our car conked out on us. The driver saw us, turned around, crossed over the median, and subsequently gave us a tow into town. I diagnosed the problem; how I did I don't even know, but it was something to do with the distributor unit. It had a broken rod in it or something. Amazingly, there was an auto parts store that had the part we needed. Thank goodness for good old Chevy 350 engines and the common motor parts. I put the part in, and after several hours of delay, we were on our way home, albeit with a slightly melted wedding cake.

I'm not sure what prompted me to agree to getting married. Well, yes I do; it was because I loved her so much, and I hoped that either my gender issues would go away or that she would somehow understand and support me in some way. Back then, I thought I should be female, but I was still doing a really good job of repressing. I hadn't spent much time thinking about it, and I still had hopes that the feelings would eventually pass. I also thought that maybe getting married would be the ticket out of my troubles. Maybe it would make a man out of me, once and for all. And maybe, if we had a child, and I really did want to have a child someday, maybe that would help me be a man, too. But at the still-young age of nineteen, little did I know. I think that if I could have known then what I know now, I might have done things differently. But in retrospect, I wouldn't change anything, because the years Cindy and I spent together were filled with many beautiful and very special times. I can't imagine having spent those times with anyone else, and I wouldn't have wanted to. And there is no way I would change anything because of our beautiful son.

It was about two years into our relationship when I told her I had gender issues—or maybe it was two years after we got married. I don't remember if I told her frankly that I had always felt I should be female or not, but I believe I did. I seem to recall she came home from work early one day to find me dressed "*en femme*," much to her dismay. At that time, she had no idea I felt this way, and from the very beginning she had an intense desire not to know about it, no matter how hard I tried to explain it to her. I took her disapproval to heart, and that encouraged me to repress the feelings even more, and deeper, than ever before. For the first time in my life, I thought I could beat it, that I could win the war inside my head, and that the thoughts and desires would leave me alone. I thought that the power of our love was stronger than anything, even me, and I believed with all my heart and soul that I, that we, could make it go away.

But it didn't. And when it would resurface it was worse than ever before. I began an absolutely mind-numbing roller-coaster ride of emotions: "I should be female." "I can overcome this." "I want to be a woman!" "But I'm married! I should be a man!" Repress. Suppress. Repress. The house is empty! Time to dig out my box of girl stuff and alleviate the pain! Oh my God, how excruciating it became. Back and forth, in and out of thoughts. Depression ensued, but I didn't want her to think it was because of her. I didn't want to hurt her. So I even repressed the depression! I became a tumultuous mess inside. Eventually, anger rose to the surface, which covered up my feelings pretty well, but not well enough. I reached a point when I realized that she had to know. She needed to understand. I needed to tell her, for my own sanity, because if I could trust anyone at all, I could trust her. Maybe she could help me!

I tried to talk to her. Tried to tell her. I begged her to help. She didn't want to acknowledge any of it. She didn't want to face it, didn't want to accept it. I think she feared that acknowledging it would lead to the current end result—that she would lose the man that she loved so dearly. I guess she was right…and for that I am eternally sorry.

Trying to Get It Together

Holding a job had always been very hard for me. In fact, doing much of anything that required a long-term effort was very hard, mainly because it was almost impossible for me to keep myself focused on things. That was a big reason for why I did so many different things all the time. I would start one project to distract myself from the constant, nagging incongruence—but it would eventually take over again, and I'd abandon that project and move on to another one. One thing I must admit is that it sure did give me a well-rounded skill set. But when it came to holding down jobs, that was a different story.

My first job was as a busser (clearing tables, filling water glasses, cleaning up) in a restaurant in the little town in Arizona where I had grown up. I worked with nice people, and there were other bussers there who were my age. I lasted a few weeks there before I quit. All I remember from that job was how shocked I was about the massive amounts of food that were wasted; the silver dollar an old man had given me for being nice to him; and how much I wished I were a girl, too, like the busgirl with whom I worked shifts.

My second job was at a major fast-food chain, and that was my first exposure to a real corporation. It was a great experience because I had an excellent boss. His name was Rich, and he was a caring and compassionate man who had a terrific sense of humor. He made working there fun, and he made it less about working for a big corporation and more about working for myself. He taught me an excellent work ethic, which has lasted to this day.

During and after college I started working odd jobs for as long as I could hold them. I worked quite a few temporary positions, doing things like cleaning theaters late at night, cleaning schools before they opened, and working as a receptionist for a long-term care office. Those were fun jobs for me because about the time I lost interest in them, they ended. I didn't have to quit or get fired. I didn't get fired from a job until I had moved to Flagstaff and got a job at the local Happy Trails head shop.

A head shop is a store that sells smoking paraphernalia,

pipes, and bongs. It was right up my alley, considering I was a long-haired guy, and it was hard for me to get a job doing much else. It seemed like everyone wanted me to cut my hair off, but I would have died before I did that.

I worked with a few other people there, most of whom were pretty cool, except for one girl who had been hired just a short time before me.

It was a week night, and the place was quiet; there were no customers at all, except for a few stragglers every hour or two. I was cutting apart some old posters the manager had set aside for me to use to make custom signage. I was making some funny signs, and when I wasn't doing that, I was cleaning the immense array of glass water pipes and other stuff behind the counter. The place looked great. In the back of the store, in the stockroom, sat my co-worker, Kim. She had set herself up at a little desk and was "studying" for a college test she had coming up, or at least that's what she had said she was doing. She had lit some incense and had the place smelling really good, but I didn't notice that she had been smoking pot while she was in there. I was hardly back there, though, and she didn't ask me if I wanted any, so I had no clue what she was doing. I didn't find out about it until the following Saturday. I also learned that she had been drinking beer back there. Talk about stupid! Who, in their right mind, smokes pot and drinks beer in a head shop of all places? Well, she was not in her right mind. Hell, maybe I was more stupid for not even noticing!

That evening, a strange couple came in. They were youngish and asked questions that I thought were rather suspicious. They spent quite a bit of time wandering around, checking things out and asking questions. With all the time they spent in the shop, I would have thought they'd have noticed I was not in the back room at all, and that Kim was. They didn't seem to care, and the reason why became perfectly clear a few days later. What really blew my mind at the time was when they went right into the office, which was locked. They had a key. I freaked out, went over to them, and said, "Who the hell are you? What do you think you're doing?" They told me that the man was Steve, one of the two owners of the company, and that the woman was his girlfriend. Both were so snotty the whole time I wondered how they could run a business. I couldn't understand why they would come in and act so rude, and not even introduce themselves to their own employees.

The next Saturday, I went to work after having had a couple of days off. When I got there, to my surprise, there were several new people working in the store. My manager, Linda, had a very troubled look on her face.

"Hey, Linda," I said as I walked in. "What's going on? Who are all these guys?" "New people," she said. "I'm sorry, Adam, I have some bad news. Come with me a minute." I had no clue what was going on. We went to the office. I can remember the moment as clearly as if it were yesterday. "I have to let you go. I'm sorry," she said. "What? Why?" I asked.

"You know I don't want to," she said. Her eyes were getting teary, and her face was gloomy. "You know how much I appreciate you and the work you do." She looked out the one-way glass at the sales floor. "Steve said you were smoking pot in the back room."

"What!" I screamed. "What the fuck! That's total bullshit!" "I know," she said.

"Linda, I would never, ever, be so stupid to do that here!" She knew I was being honest. We had a good working relationship, full of mutual respect and appreciation. I was in shock. I couldn't believe this was happening to me. I loved my job and that store. I had put everything I could into making it a cool place for people to shop, and I was suddenly without words. My eyes filled with tears. "So, what the hell," I mumbled through lips that would hardly work.

"They say they're sure you're the one who was smoking pot and drinking beer in the back room," Linda told me.

"That was Kim," I interrupted.

"I know," she said, "but they think it was you, and Kim wouldn't admit she did it. And Steve had said, 'Everyone knows it was the long-haired guy who did it.'"

I about crumpled into a ball on the floor. All that energy, all that work, all my time and effort…the long-haired guy who did it. Oh my God! How stereotypical! And that coming from former hippies and pot smokers. Wow. It was a rude awakening to the power of perception, and to how a person's appearance is perceived by others. God knows it couldn't be the cute college girl who was getting high and drunk in the back; it had to be that damn long-haired guy.

As I walked out of the store, Kim was behind the counter. I yelled across the room, so that the whole room could hear, including Steve, the owner, "What the fuck, Kim? You're letting me take the blame for something you did? Why don't you cop to it, you lying bitch!"

Steve turned to me and said, "Get the fuck out of my store." And I left, never to return, except for once, two weeks later, when I had to go pick up my paycheck. Linda told me that Kim had finally admitted the truth, and that she had been fired. Linda said she, too, was quitting and moving out of town. I guess they didn't want me back, though, which was just as well.

That was a harsh lesson learned about prejudice against me for being different. I thought it was ironic that the owner of a head shop, of all places, would make such assumptions, but I guess judgment has no regard for different types of people. I was very upset that I had been fired under such screwed-up circumstances. Being accused of something I did not do is one of the worst experiences I have ever had, but in this case there wasn't much I could do. Besides, I did not want to work for someone who would treat others like that! I moved on.

Until Cindy and I moved to Phoenix, I had little knowledge of topless bars. I was, however, aware of the places where a person could go into a booth and put a quarter in a slot; a curtain would rise, and a totally naked girl would "dance" for you in a little room. Tim and I had sneaked into a few of those once or twice. For me, the excitement was more in the act of getting in there than in watching the girls. It was kind of scary, actually, especially when I saw some creepy guy in the opposite booth doing very creepy things. One night, Tim and I managed to slip into a topless bar, the Bourbon Street Circus, but only for about fifteen minutes before we were kindly shown the way out. I found those places exciting and frustrating at the same time. On the one hand, I could see clearly what I had wanted and needed to be all my life. On the other hand, the experiences were frustrating because they were reminders of what I didn't have and who I wasn't— and the fact that I wasn't being true to myself. That's inspiration for shame and guilt, too, which just compounded the internal struggle with which I was constantly dealing.

In the mid-1980s, I desperately needed to make some money. Having long hair made it hard for me to find a job. In addition, I looked a lot younger than I really was. Looking younger than you are is a double-edged sword: I looked younger, but people treated me as if I were younger, a lot younger. To me, it felt as if they just didn't give me the respect I deserved. While I think that was true, for the most part, I'm sure my own perception also was askew, which didn't help much.

A friend of Cindy's from high school had worked in the topless clubs, and she said she was making good money. Since I was desperate for a job, it wasn't hard to decide when another friend, who had recently started working at the same club, called and said, "Hey, guess what? The deejay just walked out, and the backup isn't available. You should come to work here. I know you'd be really good at it."

"What? You mean deejay? Me?" I laughed and said no, but she talked me into it. Cindy didn't mind if I did that; she thought it might be good way to make money. We had always had a large amount of trust in each other. I went down there to the club and did my best to play the music the girls and guys wanted to hear; I did my best to have a good time, too, but I have to admit, I was scared as hell. At the end of the night, however, the girls gave me handfuls of dollar bills. They told me I kicked ass, and they wanted to work with me again. And thus began my ten-year, off-and-on career as a deejay in the Phoenix topless bar circuit.

Deejaying was a fun job that didn't require much effort, just a good knowledge of people and music. I worked at that first club for quite some time. I enjoyed everything except the smoke, the alcohol, and the people who had been drinking. Although sometimes they made for pretty good entertainment!

Cindy & Adam - late 1980's

Though it was relatively easy work, deejaying was a tough gig for me because of who I was. On the one hand, it was excruciatingly frustrating having to watch gorgeous women, gorgeous naked women, acting as sexy and seductive as possible for six or seven hours a night. All I wanted was to be just like them, but I found a way to ease my frustration and make it into a good thing. One of the interesting things about that environment is that sometimes the deejay is the only guy the girls can really talk to, so they often say things that they would not say to the customers. The bartenders don't have the time to talk, and the doormen could talk, but usually weren't much for conversation, so it was the deejay. Besides, the girls always had to interact with the deejay, so it was pretty common to be chatty. They occasionally vented, too, telling me how frustrated they were. "This guy only gave me five bucks. Five bucks!" they would say. I consoled them, but inside I thought to myself, "Oh my God, girl, if I had a body like yours, I'd own these guys!" I had always wanted to dance, just for the excitement of doing it, or for the money, but I am glad I never had the chance because there is a very high personal cost to pay for doing a job like that. It is definitely not easy, nor is it something I would recommend to any girl.

During the years I deejayed, I learned an amazing amount of information about female anatomy and physiology. I studied the way women move their bodies, their hand gestures, the way they move their heads, their ultra-feminine behaviors—and which ones worked and which ones didn't for particular body types. I learned a lot about hair and makeup, and during the final years of working in that industry, I ended up offering a lot of advice on makeup, hair, and making conversation with the guys. In many ways, I lived vicariously through the girls; if I couldn't be a dancer, I could at least help them be the best they could be. It was a good opportunity to ask them why they were there, which I did, hoping to make some roundabout suggestions that they get out. Most of them didn't, though.

There was one girl named Amber, who was only nineteen when she started. She was absolutely gorgeous. She had long maroon-colored hair, and the kind of physique I had always wanted. She was an excellent dancer, almost like a ballerina. Sometimes she was like an angel flowing around on stage. She was innocent and youthful, and I feared for her because she didn't know what she was getting herself into. I was the deejay on shift the very first time she set foot on stage.

"Are you sure you want to do this?" I asked her, after asking about her background and getting acquainted. She said she wasn't absolutely sure, but she needed some quick money to pay off her car. After that, she'd quit. Yeah, right. She and I ended up working together for two or three years after that. She raked in the money; she knew what the guys wanted, and she almost gave it to them, which was the trick of the trade. They loved her, and I was so jealous; I just wished I could look that the way she did. That was all I had ever wanted, and she was working the crowd the way I imagined that I would—if I ever had the chance.

A few years later, after I had been out of the business, Cindy, Anvil, and I were at Kay-bee Toys in the mall. We were looking for toys for Anvil. I turned and saw a bleached-blond woman wrangling two young kids, who were about four or five years old. She looked awfully familiar, and so did the man with her, who was paying for some toys. I moved around to get a better view of her face; it was Amber.

"Amber?" I said as I walked up to her. She turned to face me; her body was skinny, and her face was nearly emaciated. Her eyes were sunken, and dark rings filled in the space where once beautiful, supple cheeks had been. There was tiredness in her eyes, and a lost loneliness in them, too. She tried to smile when she recognized me, but her face couldn't mask her pain.

"Adam?" she said, "Wow…" She tried to talk to me but couldn't really think of much to say. Her husband, who had been a regular customer of hers, turned around with a bag of toys in his hand. I said hello to him and told Amber I'd see her around. She said it was good to see me, but I couldn't bring myself to say the same to her, for it ripped my heart out. "Take care of yourself," I said, and I turned and left.

I'm not sure what happened to her—drugs, sickness, exhaustion, or what. But the gorgeous young ballerina I had met only a few years before was gone. I was glad I wasn't in that industry anymore. Working in the clubs isn't necessarily bad, but one has to be very strong to deal with all the things that come along with it. In the end, I am thankful that I had the opportunity to work in those clubs, and with so many neat people. There were lots of not-so-neat people, too, but the memories of them have drifted away with the smoke and stench from the bar.

Meeting Amber again was profound in that it really got me thinking about how the choices people make affect them. I consciously mulled over my own options. What would I become if I were to try to change? What will happen to me if I don't change? Will I survive either way? I concluded that I was basically fucked, to put it bluntly, but that's exactly how I felt. I didn't feel as if I had any options, not the way Amber had. She had options. She could have chosen a different path, couldn't she have? Well, after contemplating that, I wasn't so sure. Maybe we're all just destined for whatever we're destined for. So that was that. I was destined to be trapped. To be punished for…for what exactly? I didn't even know. I was becoming more and more lost within my own being. My head said one thing; my body displayed another. My self-worth plummeted and depression was only a thought or feeling away. But it was so important to keep up appearances, to hide how frustrated and confused I had become, to show what a man I was by not revealing my deepest emotions. Repression, my lonely friend until the end, I will die with you…you and I…so alone…so utterly…purely…alone. The black veil of darkness loomed over me once again.

There were so many moments like that, when I just dropped down into dark self-loathing and self-hatred. It came out in bursts of anger from time to time, but never at anyone else; my anger was always directed at myself or at inanimate objects, like my car steering wheel, my computer keyboard, or the mouse. As time went on, and especially after I learned about and began to understand what my issue was, I became increasingly frustrated because I knew that there really was something I could do about my problem. That was, of course, to change. In my heart, that is what I really wanted to do. It's what I had always wanted to do. Since my first memories, I had always just wanted to be me, to be the girl I should have been all along. Here I was again, feeling sorry for myself, and that was driving me crazy.

Not all my waking hours were spent in depression, of course. I had many days that were smooth, when I enjoyed my life and being with Cindy and Anvil. They were what helped me through, although they didn't know it at the time. I lived for them, and through them, through their happiness, I was happy. I tried to do whatever I could to be the perfect father, the perfect husband, but my heart, that heart that knew the truth, kept getting in my way. What could I do to stop that? It was right inside the middle of me! Tear it out! But no, I could not. I had to endure. I had to deal with my pain. I had to hide myself away, from Cindy, from Anvil, from myself. One half of me forced the thoughts away…one half of me fought to break free, fought to survive. Sometimes it seemed as if I were playing a sick game with myself—forcing myself to suffer for the pleasure I was receiving. Suffering for the happiness of my family. Suffering to keep them from embarrassment and shame.

Endure

Cut into the deepest part of me
Release to set myself free
Feel pain—to relieve pain—Endure
Seek pain—to release pain—Endure
Tear away the skin that keeps it all inside

Crawl out of the shell to become alive
Need pain—to relieve pain—Endure
Feed pain—to decrease pain—Endure
The sweet flavor of steel inside
The smell of open flesh
Bodies begin to writhe
Pain and pleasure mesh
The putrid smell of the City streets
The luscious torture of a million souls
Nothing more than a flock of sheep
In a beautiful, trashed and burned-out world
We must endure—So we can live

I Am the Rock. I Am the Hard Place.

As always, our main focus was each other, as well as music and finding decent jobs. I was working on trying to make art a career, as well. I applied for a few different art-related jobs, but never heard back. I did not follow up though, which I should have. It was a financially tough time for us, but our life together was good and we were deeply in love and enjoying each other very much. My incongruence would wax and wane every few months it seemed. I could keep it at bay for a while, then it would return with a vengeance. I found myself looking forward to having time alone at home so I could dress and find some time to relax. Though it helped, it was never enough.

During the late 1980s Cindy met a girl named Lynn at a club where they both worked. Lynn mentioned to Cindy that her husband, Rudy, played bass and was heavily into Metallica and Slayer. He was starting to look for musicians to form a band. Cindy told Lynn that I played guitar and was also into Metallica, and they decided that it would be a good idea if Rudy and I got together to make some musical noise.

One evening, Cindy and I drove over to Lynn and Rudy's apartment. We introduced ourselves, and I set up my guitar and amp. Rudy seemed like a pretty cool guy; he was tall and skinny, with long dark brown/black hair and a goatee. He looked like a blend of Jesus and Jafar, the evil character from the animated movie *Aladdin*. He hardly seemed evil, though. In fact, he was charismatic, intelligent, and a cool guy overall. We got along well enough, and we tried to play some songs together, but it didn't really work out very well at the time because of the gap in our experience levels.

We played together only a few times, and then we parted ways for a year or so. There wasn't any particular reason other than we were just busy with our own lives, I guess.

As our early years passed, we had many good times just being with each other. There were moments when we both agreed that we didn't need anything else in life, for we had each other, and that was all we ever needed. I worked. Cindy went to Arizona State, we practiced music and stayed as creative as we could. Life was good, but tough for me, considering I had been doing a good job repressing my feelings and the better I did that, and the longer I did it, the more power they would have when they would emerge again. I coped by unearthing my stash of clothes, which I kept hidden from Cindy in an old box full of electronic parts and old guitar cords and junk. Those brief moments of relief usually came when Cindy was at work, which often resulted in feeling somewhat guilty when she returned home. I felt like I was doing something sneaky and wrong, but that was only because I didn't think she would approve of it. In hindsight, I think that guilt was unjustified, all things considered.

Soon, the thoughts of having a baby came to mind. We talked about it, debated whether or not we should or shouldn't. At one point we agreed, why should we bring a child into this crazy world, and we decided against it. After some more time had passed, though, we began to think about it again and discuss it further. Then we decided that if we were going to have a child, we should probably do it sooner rather than later, and about a year later, in 1991, Anvil was born.

I will never forget watching the top of his head emerge. I stood next to Cindy, holding her hand in mine, and gripping the railing on the edge of the hospital bed with my other. My knees became like ice, and I could barely stand up. I was in awe. My life was changing before my eyes. And minutes later our son was born. It was one of the best moments in my life. I've cherished it since the minute it happened, and I will continue to cherish it until my memories escape into the ether with the energy that is my life. In those precious moments, as I gazed at the beautiful new life we had created, I had no idea how much my life would change. It changed for the better, and not a day goes by that I don't think about how much I love my baby, and how thankful I am that we had him and that he is in this world with us.

The following several years were very hard for me because of the gender issues. I had many dark moments when I would consciously fight it, working hard to repress it. I thought I had so much to lose if I let it out, if I let myself out, yet it was impossible to keep it bottled up. As I repressed my feelings of gender incongruence, the energy seemed to have a will of its own and a determination to come out of me in one way or another. The main method it seemed to choose was the form of anger, and it always came out at the most stressful times.

One day I was working on my car and Anvil, then about two years old, was sitting with me, watching. I was trying to change my brakes, trying to get the front caliper off, and my wrench slipped. I smashed my knuckles on a grimy bolt, leaving my hand black and dripping blood. I cursed the car and tried again, and slipped again, this time unleashing a fury of rage at the car, smashing the fender into a mess with a  hammer, screaming my frustration at the car, not solely because my hand hurt, but more because I wasn't allowing myself to be. When I realized that Anvil had been watching me unleash my wrath upon the car, I reached a critical turning point and had one of several epiphanies that proved crucial to bringing me closer to resolving my dilemma. Over the course of the next few years, I worked very hard to get away from my anger, and I did a very good job of moving beyond it.

The main method I used to move through my anger was research and self-help. I read voraciously, spending a lot of time at the library and studying everything I could find. Eventually, these years of study lead me to a logical conclusion: to resolve my anger, I had to take care of the root cause of the anger. It did not take long to realize exactly what that was, and it wasn't what I wanted to admit. I figured there were two ways to deal with it: Keep repressing and try to cope in other ways, or fix the problem so I would not have the feelings of gender dysphoria anymore, which meant changing my sex. But we had just had a child, and we were a happy family. I couldn't change my sex. So I tried to go with the alternative.

As always, music continued to be an outlet for me and I spent a lot of time focused on my guitar and writing and recording music. Cindy was aspiring to sing and we looked around for a bass player and drummer for a short time. We found an okay bass player and tried to get a band together, but it just didn't work out. I kept working crappy jobs, like washing dishes at restaurants, and later at a sports bar. One thing about working at the sports bar that was cool was that there was often down time when I waited for dishes to come back to the wash area. I used to write a lot of song lyrics and poems back there, and those always helped me cope with my issues very well.

Each year we went down to Yuma to visit Cindy's mom, grandparents, and other family, for Thanksgiving. Those times still stand as some of my all-time favorite memories from the years we were together. Cindy's brother would come over from California, too,  and her mom's house was always packed full of people. We'd spend the day helping make food and then, of course, eating it and slipping into a "food coma". This picture of Anvil, me and our Whippet, Jasper, is from one of those Thanksgiving visits. Those times were nice distractions from everyday life, struggling to survive financially, struggling with internal issues, but still, I fought and fought my constant feelings of incongruence, no matter where I was. It was becoming a stronger and stronger force and consuming more and more of my mental energy.

One day, Lynn was in the area and came over to visit. As it turned out, Rudy and a guy named Chris had started a heavy metal band (without a name) and were rehearsing with a stand-in drummer just around the corner from our condo.

Lynn said, "They're practicing right now. You should go check them out." So we all headed over there. They were practicing in a rented ministorage unit, and it was loud inside. I met Chris, and the drummer, and I think it was Lynn who told them I played guitar, too. They got excited and told me to go get my stuff, so I went home, got my gear, and set it up. We played through some Metallica songs, and all of us were awed by the chemistry we had. All we needed was a name, and a good drummer.

Time passed, and we got better and better, although we had a hard time finding drummers who could play our heavy style. Our original songs were very heavy metal, sometimes very fast and sometimes melodic and dark. We needed a drummer who had a unique style and who could play weird timings to be our foundation. We found a really awesome drummer, Jeff, who was solid and had a lot of experience. The only problem was that he was into a different kind of music than we were, so it wasn't working quite right. He stuck with us for a little while, though, until we found a replacement.

One night, after one of our rehearsals, Jeff had taken off already, and we noticed this guy with long scraggly hair who was hanging around the storage unit, checking us out. He was Craig, the boyfriend of one of Lynn's friends, and she and he had come down to check us out. Evidently he'd been drinking quite a bit, and so the first time any of us met him he was stumbling through our practice area, slurring his speech as he talked about how tight our band was, and how much we needed a better drummer.

"You guys really need a better drummer," he slurred, with a big, shit-eating grin on his face.

"Oh really?" we asked.

"Yeah…" he said.

"You know of one?" we asked.

"Yeah…" he drawled, trying to make a half-sly smile.

"Who?" we asked.

"Me!" he said, gleaming. We all laughed and said, "Yeah, right!" But we had to admit, he totally looked like a drummer. And, well, he was acting like one, too. Then he said he wanted to show us, and he got on Jeff's kit. Even though he was drunk, he pounded out some incredible drum work. It impressed us all very much, and we told him, "Look, you can come back when you're sober and try out, but until then, get off the drumset." He was so happy he was glowing. It was a great night that I'll never forget.

A few days later, we tried him out, and it didn't take long for us to decide he was our new drummer. I think it only took us the first few bars of "Seek and Destroy" to decide that. He blew us away, and we inducted him into the band. Our band, although still nameless, was complete.

We practiced by playing some Metallica songs, and then we began to write our own stuff. Once we had enough songs together, we started looking to play shows, but first we needed a name for the band. At the time, I was working for a local computer furniture store. I would assemble and deliver office/computer furniture to businesses and homes. I enjoyed it a lot because I got to travel around and experience different places. One day, while I was driving north past the desert hills, I saw a lone thunderstorm in the desert mountains near the horizon. It was very cool because it was pretty much the only set of clouds in the sky. Within the dark gray puffs and the flow of rain dropping from them there were occasional bursts of lightning. It was beautiful, and I wished I could hear the thunder, because that is one of my most favorite sounds. As I drove and watched the little storm, I thought about thunder, and thundering music, and about how I wanted our band to just rule. The name for the band struck me: Thunderin' Reign. The next time we practiced, I suggested the name, and everyone was in total agreement that this should be the name of the band, and so it was.

We worked hard for a long time and had about twelve songs in our repertoire, most of which were originals. Chris and I swapped lead vocal duties, but he was strictly a rhythm guitarist, so I took all the solos. The four of us worked

really well together, and after we got our live set organized, we began playing shows in and around Phoenix, not the least of which were two times when we opened for the then notso-well-known band Tool.

After Thunderin' Reign had been together a year or two, we had already played quite a few shows at the most popular Phoenix rock/metal club called the Mason Jar. Franco, the owner, seemed to like us, and he really liked that we could play Metallica stuff so well. One night, before one of our gigs there, he asked if we would put on a "Metallica Tribute" show. I told him and the band that I didn't think it was such a good idea because we'd get pigeonholed as a "Metallicover" band. The guys tentatively agreed, but Franco insisted that we do the show he had in mind.

So I said, "All right, we'll do this show of yours if you give us an opening slot before a really good national band."

"Oh," Franco said hesitantly, in his thick Italian accent, "Okay…let's go look at the calendar." He looked at the current month and mumbled, "No…" Then he flipped to the next month and mumbled, "No…" As he began turning to the next month, I noticed "Tool" marked on the square for June 23, and I blurted, "Hey wait! That's it! Tool! We'll do the Tool show on the 23rd."

Franco laughed and said, "Oh? Ha ha! Nope. No way. You guys can't do that show."

"Oh really?" I said. "Fine then." And I started walking out of his office.

"Oh, okay…" he said, "Okay, okay. You can open for Tool."

I must have jumped through the ceiling with excitement! I was so thrilled it was indescribable. Craig was into Tool at the time, too, and he was as elated as I was. Chris and Rudy hadn't heard Tool yet, so they were just standing there, quizzically observing as all this went down.

June 23 came along so incredibly slowly, but it finally arrived. We had lugged our gear to the club and were hanging out, pre-staging our stuff. There was a tour bus, which belonged to Tool, parked outside the club, but we hadn't yet seen any of the band members around. But while I was helping Craig set up his drum set outside the back door of the club, Maynard, the enigmatic singer for Tool, walked around the corner. He looked at us as he walked past us, and he sat down along the wall several yards away from us.

"Dude!" I said to Craig. "That's Maynard!" Craig looked, and his eyes popped open. Maynard sat leaning against the wall, with his arms around his knees, and looked over at us with a "fuck you" kind of expression on his face.

"Dude, check this out…" Craig said to me as I put one of his cymbals on its stand. "I'm gonna play part of 'Hush.'"

"Oh, no, dude," I warned him. "Don't do that! He'll slay you with his evil eye!" Even as I was saying this, Craig started playing a very recognizable drum part from "Hush," one of the songs from Tool's first album. I watched Maynard's reaction as Craig played. He looked over at Craig as if he were hexing him, stood up, and walked over to the marquee; he leaned against it for a minute, then disappeared until Tool took the stage a couple of hours later. I was embarrassed, but Craig thought it was really funny.

Later, Cindy and I found Danny Carey, Tool's drummer, hanging out, and she and I spoke to him for a while. He was cool and very down-to-earth. He had already become my favorite drummer, but after talking to him I held him in even higher regard.

The show went well. We played well, and I had such a great time, especially during one of the songs I had written, called "Bitter End." I have footage of our band for this show, and of me singing this song. It was a song I wrote about what I was going through with my gender issues, even though at the time I didn't know exactly what I was dealing with. The words go like this:

Bitter End

I have a strange addiction, like something I can't control
It's something that I want no part in—anymore
This feeling grips my brain, like some nightmare's monster
And then when I think I'm sane—it starts all over
I have the strangest feeling, like I've been here before
I've gotta stop this madness—I can't take any more
I'm the only one in control, of my own mind
I know there's some way out—that's what I'll find
Now that I've cleared out my brain, I can take control
I'll be thinkin' on my own again—forever more
My friend, do you know this feeling?
Can you see your bane?
Yeah, I can see it in his eyes—he's insane!

After we played, we stuck around and watched Tool play. It was very cool to see them perform. There weren't that many people at that show, so I was right at the front of the stage to watch them. In all, I'd say it was one of the most fun shows I've had the pleasure of performing at. Not only did we play that show with them, but we also opened for them again when they came back through Phoenix on July 31. The club was absolutely packed full of people for that show. All this was shortly before their album, *Undertow*, was released. I still kick myself in the butt for not videotaping them that night!

We continued on and played a number of other shows around the valley, struggling to make our way toward rock stardom, but it wasn't in the cards for Thunderin' Reign. Sadly, because of reasons unknown to any of us, Craig took his life in mid-1993.

Craig had this kind of funky black widow tattoo on the inside of one of his wrists, which he proudly showed me one day. He made sure to point out the scar that divided the tattoo in half, leaving two halves of a spider, separated by an eighth-inch-wide scar. He said, "See that line? That's where I cut my wrist." I asked if he had done it intentionally, and he answered yes. I asked him what the hell was up with that, and he said he tried to kill himself but he didn't cut deep enough. Then he laughed. I said, "Oh, that's fucking stupid, dude! You're not gonna try to kill yourself again, are you? That would suck!" He assured me he would not.

Craig must have had some deep, unresolved issues—we all knew that, especially later on, but we didn't know what they were. He never said anything about it to any of us. I had some thoughts, but I wrote them off. One night, he and his fiancée had an argument at their house. He shot a gun into a wall. No one was hurt. She took their baby and left. Cops arrived. He was outside on the back patio with a gun in one hand, and cops were all around the backyard. They told him to drop it. He didn't. They warned him again. He laughed at them, so they shot him with rubber bullets, trying to get him to drop the gun. But instead he put the barrel in his mouth…and pulled the trigger.

There were a lot of people at his funeral, and they had an open casket. I walked up to it. He lay there, motionless. I touched his shoulder. It was cold…and hard. His face was all wrong, but it was he. His hair was unmistakable. We put some drumsticks in with him, and I gave him one of my guitar picks. He didn't move, but I wanted him to sit up and laugh; because he had always been a silly guy. But he just lay there, still as a rock, such a harsh contrast to the animated and silly person he had been. It wasn't fair. It just wasn't right! I slipped into a walking coma, devastated by the suicide of another friend. Cindy and I went home and lay on our bed, staring at the ceiling for the longest time. I can see that moment as if it were this morning. And the pain feels almost as fresh now as it did back then. Dammit, Craig! Why?

Craig's dramatic departure from our lives, and from our band, left us musically and emotionally incapacitated for quite some time. It took us months just to get back to the point where we thought we could start looking for a new drummer. We tried out several, but none of them could play the intricate and oddly timed stuff we were doing, at which Craig had become a master. Our band fell apart. We fell apart. It all just hurt too much: our friend was dead and our band was being ground to a screeching halt. Without him with us…there was this gaping, open, bleeding, throbbing wound that we couldn't mend, no matter how hard we tried. Every time we tried out another drummer it was like ripping that wound open again and shoving a bunch of salt into it, grinding it in. Eventually, Chris quit the band and I followed suit soon after. Our hearts were broken, and our impetus was shattered. We drifted apart, and that was the end of Thunderin' Reign.

I packed my guitars away and stored them in my closet. Two years passed before I would pull them out and begin playing again.

Catalysts for Change

When I was about thirty-two years old, the realization dawned on me again: I wasn't living my life. I wasn't seeing me in the mirror, and by then I knew why, for the most part. But just knowing is one thing; accepting it is a completely different challenge altogether. Funny how you can keep realizing the same thing, over and over again, but fail to accept it. The problem was obvious to me: I was supposed to be female, and I wasn't. For some strange reason, I knew this was how I felt, but it was very hard to accept it consciously. All my life, I had dealt with this conundrum, mostly by being confused and scared by it. So in my early thirties, I began to contemplate my situation seriously, and I started to take a detailed look at who I was, where I'd been, where I was headed, what was going on inside my head, and what was happening to my life's path. I took a long, hard look at what I needed in order to be happy with my life. I pictured myself at the end of my life and asked myself if I would truly be happy if I kept going down the road I was on. When I came to the answer to that question, it was like jumpstarting a car, I was finally on my way to becoming myself— for the first time in my life. Even though I was armed with that knowledge, I still found it almost impossible to make the changes I needed to make. I felt that there was just too much at stake, and I was very, very scared of losing everything. In times like that, we just need some kind of trigger, some sort of "kick in the pants" to get us motivated. We need something that will cause the desire to change to outweigh our fears of change. We need a catalyst.

For every action there is an equal and opposite reaction. This is, of course, Sir Isaac Newton's Third Law of Motion. Mr. Newton's actions are still felt today. His Third Law of Motion applies to us as well as it does to anything else in the universe. Often there is this "thing," this feeling, pressing inside us, begging to get out. It is hard to think about it objectively since it is "all in our heads"; it is very subjective. That is, however, only one way to look at it—it is not so much "in our heads" as it is of our flesh; since we cannot change our heads, the only recourse is to change our bodies. Medical research is continuing to support the theory that transsexualism is caused by biological circumstances beyond our control and that treatments using same-sex hormones, hypnotherapy, electroshock therapy, lobotomies or other "mind-changing" methods cannot remedy the situation. But it has been proven time and time again that changing the body to match the mind does work, and people like me are living proof of that.

Sometimes we don't even need to take the first step on our own. Sometimes there are external forces that cross our paths, act on us, and cause us to react.

A few years after Thunderin' Reign had dissolved, Cindy and I found ourselves looking for some kind of direction in our lives, and for some kind of control over our financial situation. We became involved in Amway, of all things, mostly "for the good prices" but also because we wanted to try to make some money. We didn't realize that there really wasn't much money to be made in it, although it was mildly entertaining trying. And I must admit, the tapes they had about selling, being positive, and how to negotiate were very enlightening.

Part of the Amway process is to make a list of everyone you have ever known and to scratch their names off the list once you have contacted them to give them the Amway presentation. On that list were our long-departed friends and band co-conspirators, Rudy and Lynn. They were, in fact, the very last two people on the list.

"You call them," Cindy said.

"No, I don't want to. You do it," I said.

She procrastinated just long enough for me to say, "Okay, fine! I'll do it."

I still remember looking at the phone and thinking that I shouldn't call them, but I did, and they were still at  the same number. Rudy answered the phone. We said the usual hellos, and I told him we had something cool to share. He didn't seem very interested in that, but invited us over to their house to get together and catch up.

We drove to their house, which was only a few miles away, and as we pulled up in front of it, I wondered if anyone actually lived there. The yard was dead looking, as though it hadn't been watered in years, which it probably hadn't. The bushes were all dead, and there were cobwebs all over the entry way. Thinking back on it, that was actually rather appropriate, considering how things turned out. We walked up to the door and knocked; both Cindy and I were very nervous, to say the least.

Lynn answered the door, beautiful and glowing, as she almost always was. She was, and is, such a healthy and vibrant woman, with not an ounce of fat on her, and in great physical shape with stunning looks, like Gina Gershon and Cindy Crawford. She was absolutely gorgeous.

She welcomed us in, and we entered their living room, which was beautifully adorned with candles, paintings, and porcelain figurines of dolphins and dragons. There were pretty pieces of fabric for decoration, incense burners, and pictures of family members. It was a very warm and inviting place to be, friendly and cozy. We sat on the big, cushy couch. Rudy joined us, and the four of us sat and began talking about what we had been up to for the past few years since the band had broken up. We never got the opportunity to show them our Amway tape, which was probably just as well. I am sure they would not have had any interest whatsoever.

To fully understand this chapter in my life, you need to understand Rudy a bit more. His methods and intentions have been, shall we say, a bit askew from the norm. Many might say he's downright evil, and even I have said that, but the more time that has passed, the less I feel that way. In fact, I have felt neutral about him after moving away from Phoenix. Since I had last seen him when the band broke up, he had taken on a far more charismatic quality and what his purpose lacked in logic, his charisma made up for tenfold. But since we had once been band mates, and I still considered him a friend, it was hard for me to realize just how much he had changed. I had no idea what was in store for us.

As we sat on their couch talking, or listening, rather, Cindy and I were wondering if we would ever get the chance to show them our video. Rudy had already begun working on us, with his subtle and manipulative ways. He was a master manipulator, so people were easily drawn into what he was saying. The basic premise of his idea was something he called "Best Path." It is based on his own ideas of an apocalyptic demise of earth and humanity, and the need for certain souls to be on Best Path in order to survive the apocalypse. From the very first moment he began telling us about this, I was skeptical, as I have always been about such subjects, and it would have taken quite a bit of convincing to make me believe in anything so farfetched. At that time, I was in a desperate place in my life, with confusion over gender dysphoria running rampant in me, and Cindy was in a place in life where she was looking for something more. We were both in need of something, anything that might help us to get ourselves together. So, in the standard Best Path way, we said yes to Best Path—saying yes to things that were asked of you was very important to the manipulation process—and thus began a very long and very challenging time in both our lives.

It seemed harmless enough. We went to the house every Sunday and participated with about ten people in a "circle," which mostly consisted of Rudy telling us about current events and how Best Path was working to help us all get over our personal issues so we would be "cleansed" for when the apocalypse came. I laugh about it now, and I was laughing about it then, just not externally. During the circles we read tarot cards, or I should say Rudy read them. He would interpret them in any way he thought would work best for his manipulations, and they were often very powerful tools for making others believe that he had mystic powers.

Telling the future was a big part of his game. In fact, he was a self-proclaimed psychic and claimed he could teleport his astral self anywhere in the known and unknown universe. That always tickled me, and I often found it hard not to burst out laughing. I think I may have actually done that once or twice. Many times, something political or newsworthy would happen, such as the death of someone in a position of power, and he would claim that he had psychically teleported there and had killed the person. How any of us ever stuck around after hearing stuff like that is beyond me. I must admit, though, it was good for the entertainment value alone; you never knew what to expect from him. But it was not worth the risk.

One of the main parts of Best Path was the process of "cleansing" our psyches of the "bad programs" we had. These were negative mental frameworks that needed rectifying, and it was imperative that they be removed completely so that those of us on the Best Path could survive the apocalypse. Rudy made it a point to find out exactly what our bad programs were; that was a strong focus for him, and a strong psychological leverage, too. He used that against us all the time. My negative program was not what you might think: it wasn't that I was transsexual, but rather that I was angry. Many of the negative programs were based on the seven deadly sins, something he also used as a psychological tool to take advantage of others.

The main tenet of the cleansing process was that all our problems were caused by our parents, and it was important for us to close those circles, which involved confronting our parents. My mission was to drive to California and to blame Dad for all my problems in life. I hate to even think about this now, let alone write about it, but I did that. I drove six hours to my parents' house, and while Dad was working in his garage, I blamed him for everything—for my anger issues and for whatever was wrong with me. He was shocked, to say the least, and he was angry, which he had the right to be. I didn't say anything to him, or to Mom, about being transsexual, and I surely did not blame them for that. In fact, I really didn't blame them for anything, even the things I was standing there blaming him for. I was doing it under the influence of Best Path. Even though I thought it wasn't affecting me, I had begun to. It was at least two years before I would talk to Mom and Dad again.

To this day, I wish I had not done that. It hurt my parents so deeply, and they did not deserve to hear such mean accusations from their child. Sometimes I wonder how they have ever forgiven me for that, but perhaps it is their understanding and compassion that has helped them to forgive.

One day I decided to test Rudy's psychic abilities. I asked him what my real problem was.

"Anger," he said.

"Anger, huh?" I said, in deep contemplation. "Anger at what?" "What do you mean?" he asked.

"Why am I angry?" I asked.

"You are angry because of your father," he said. For some reason the thought of Darth Vader and Luke Skywalker came to mind. I almost laughed.

"Because of my father?" I asked.

"Yes; his anger is manifested in you," he said.

"No, I don't think that's quite it," I said. "Anger is not a cause; it is a symptom."

"No," he said. "Anger is your sin. That is what you need to overcome."

"But can't you see the real cause for my anger?" I asked him, implying that his psychic skills should be able to determine that. He just studied me quietly, and then changed the subject.

It was then that I knew, for sure, that he was full of crap. I was already sure, but I had wanted to test him. If he were aware that I was testing him, his argument would surely be that he knew I was testing him, and he therefore played along. But who knows, and who really cares? People will either believe in that kind of thing or they won't. Personally, I don't, and after that experience, I doubt I ever will. It wasn't until after about two years of being involved with them that I finally told the whole group, during a circle gathering, what was really causing my anger. But there was a lot of intense stuff that led up to that.

One of the interesting things about Rudy was that he never left the house. They lived in a standard, ranch-style house in Phoenix, and he hadn't worked in years. He just sat around inside the house, preaching his Best Path gospel and brainwashing people. Perhaps he was agoraphobic, I don't know. Poor Lynn had to work her butt off to support him, herself, and a number of others who lived at the house with them. Rudy forced her to do that, and he made her support everyone financially. He also made their roommates, most of them female, do the work around the house. He said it was their duty for Best Path. One time, one of them crossed Best Path, actually crossed Rudy, and he made her do housework in the nude, whipping her with a leather riding crop when she didn't obey. He forced the women staying with them to have sex with him, in the name of Best Path. He made Lynn recruit new girls through her work to be part of the group. Some came and went, and some stayed. From what I understand, one of them is still with Rudy, but Lynn, bless her soul, left him a couple of years after I was kicked out.

One day, toward the end of my experience with Best Path, Rudy told me that because they had only one car, and we had two, that I needed to give my truck to Lynn so that she could make money to support my family. She had recently moved out of the house, not of her own free will, but because Best Path said so, and she had been forced to leave their one car with Rudy, or really, with the girls who were living in the house with him. Thus, it was my duty to Best Path to give her my truck because we only need one vehicle.

"Uhh...No," I said. "I need my truck to get to work. Without it, I can't get to work, so that's not going to happen." That was true, but I also did not like him ordering me to do things; it was way outside of reason, and I was pretty pissed that he was demanding this and, even worse, demanding it under the guise of some phony mystic mumbo-jumbo.

"Well," he said, "if you want to stay on Best Path, then you'll give your truck to Lynn." I was astonished!

"No," I said.

"Then Best Path doesn't want you around here until you give her your truck," he commanded. "You're banned from the house until then. You may not call here, either."

"Oh really?" I yelled from across the room, "Fine! Fuck this then!" And I left. Cindy was still there, but she had driven over in our other car.

I went home, broke down, and cried for quite some time. A little while later, Cindy and one of the girls from the house came by, and Cindy began collecting some of her stuff. She told me that she was moving up to Rudy's house for a little while, and that I was going to have to take care of Anvil at our house in the meantime. I was working and didn't know any babysitters, so this development threw quite the monkey wrench at me. I was in shock over what was going on in my life; I just watched her pack a few things and leave.

As if the challenge of dealing with gender incongruence wasn't enough, now everything I held dear seemed to be falling to pieces.

The next several days were hell for me. I did the best I could with Anvil, but when it came time for me to go to work where I was deejaying, I had to call in sick because I could not find anyone to watch him. Everyone we knew, at that time in our lives, was part of Best Path, so I was somewhat screwed in the social department. I called in once more. The second time I called, I was told I didn't need to come back. I had gotten fired. No big surprise there, and I wasn't too bummed about not having a job anymore, but with everything else that was going on, in my life and in my head, I became a mess, to say the least.

My days became a torrent of emotion. I had been journaling my feelings and experiences already and that had helped me some, but it wasn't enough at the time. Things were heavy, very heavy. Poor Anvil was trying to enjoy each day and grow, and here we were, caught up in this horrible mess. I felt like such a failure, as a person and as a parent. I got depressed, more depressed than I had ever been in my life, more depressed than I could ever have imagined I could be. I felt so utterly hopeless, so extremely worthless, useless, and good for nothing—I couldn't even provide for my family. I had alienated my own parents, for two years at that point, and what kind of crappy child had I become? I was pathetic, and there was no reason for my existence. I had just about hit the very bottom.

I remember that day so vividly still. Anvil was asleep in his room. He was a little cherub lying there, so beautiful, so serene, a little star in a sea of blackness. I kissed his cheek, smelled his soft hair, told him I loved him more than life itself, and went back into our bedroom. I took my 9mm semiautomatic pistol out of its case and stared at it for a while. I loaded the clip with one bullet. I racked the slide and stared at the pistol in my hands. "One purpose for this thing," I mumbled miserably to myself, "just one. Just this one purpose—to take life away, to take my life away."

Anvil moaned, and I heard the sound of him moving around. I was jolted from my nightmare for a moment, put the gun back in its case, and put the case back in the closet. Then when I went into the living room Anvil was standing there. He asked me what I was doing, and I told him I didn't know. My face must have been swollen from crying; my eyes hurt, and my face was wet with tears. I grabbed him, hugged him, and told him I loved him so much. A few minutes later, I picked up the phone and, against the will of Best Path, I called Rudy's house. Cindy answered.

"Hello?" she asked.

"It's me…" I mumbled weakly.

"I can't talk to you," she whispered.

"I'm…I…" I stumbled over my words, over my thoughts, "I can't do this. I can't make it. I want to die, Cindy. I want to die! I just want this pain to go away.

I can't take it anymore." The phone was silent.

"I…" she started.

"Who the fuck is that!?" Rudy's voice boomed from the background. "Is that

Adam?"

"Yes," she said to him.

"Hang up the phone," he said. "Hang it up, now."

"I have to go," she said meekly. "Good-bye." And she hung up.

I dropped the phone to the floor. My head was devoid of anything, everything. I watched the phone bounce around on the hardwood floor as if it were in slow motion. It finally found a place to be still, and I thought I needed to do the same. Then I looked up at Anvil, who was standing there with a look of concern on his face. He came to me and hugged me. Although I thought that all the last traces of hope were lost, they were not, because my last bit of hope was squeezing me as hard as he could and holding on to me so I couldn't go. He saved my life at that moment, and I don't think he even knows it. But there were still even worse moments to come, when again all hope seemed to disappear.

Cindy showed up about a half hour later, fully charged with the wrath of Best Path. Rudy had told her to come to the house to kick me out of it, which she had somehow worked up the courage to do. She came in the door and told me to leave. "Get out!" she yelled. "No! This is my house!" I yelled back. But in the end, maybe I wanted to leave. At least then I knew I could go end my misery and pain in peace and quiet and not bother the ones I loved with my bloody corpse. I grabbed the nearest cardboard box and stuffed a few clothes in it. I put my journal in the box. I got my acoustic guitar, and I put it and my gun in there, too.

My face was swollen. My chest hurt. My head was spinning. My eyes were so puffy I could hardly see. I threw the box into my truck, while Cindy kept yelling, "Go! Get out of here!" I kept trying to ask her why she was doing this, why she hated me so much, but my throat was stuck; I could do nothing but crawl like a wretch into the driver's seat and try to drive away from the two people I loved most in the world.

I got about a quarter of a mile away from the house and had to pull over. My eyes were so filled with tears and were so swollen that I couldn't even see the road. I tried to figure out which would be the best choice: drive my truck into a concrete wall, drive out to the desert and shoot myself, or smash head-on into a semi or something. The last one was definitely out; I didn't want to hurt anyone else—I just couldn't do that. The second one was out because I couldn't be sure I'd die in a crash like that, and the first one…well, when I started picturing doing that to myself, all I could see was the face of my little baby, my sweet baby boy, my cherub, my angel, my life saver. And I realized again that there was no way at all that I could ever kill myself. I just couldn't do that to my baby boy! I just couldn't leave him, and I couldn't make him live a life in which his father left him behind so harshly, so coldly. I had to survive, if for nothing or no one else but for my boy. If Cindy didn't need me, and I didn't need me, then my son sure did! My son needed me!

My whole body ached. My head was pounding, and my heart was, too. I knew I couldn't go back to the house, and I had nowhere else to go. I was so alone, or was I? Circles. Circles needing closure. My parents. I needed them now more than ever, and they needed me. I owed them the biggest apology ever, and I owed it to them now. If there was one thing I actually did learn from the whole Best Path experience, it was that circles really do need closure, but not in a negative or blaming way. Circles needed closure in a positive and loving way, and that became my goal from then on: to find peace within myself, to take care of me, and to find and be me, for the first time in my life, and for the rest of my life. And the first thing I needed to do was to apologize to Mom and Dad.

The Eagle Cries

If I could halt raging rains, I would but let them pour
Instead raising my strength with forgiveness to darkened skies
To let it be as it should be and buck it nevermore
As do echoes relinquished by soaring eagle's cries
Tenfold times three and three but more I have dwelt in banished halls
Borne in silence, solace, and waxing glimpses of agony
Ageless seems this fire within my soul sounds of hammer falls
Unto stilled bell within my heart doth ring now profoundly
Alive the word for which I live in moments each a precious gem
Earned by strength in forgiveness now to my own self I let pour
Value of which cannot be drawn nor held within the hand
Let not life slip through wretched fingers and drop upon the floor
If I could halt raging rains, I would but let them pour
Instead stand tall beside myself arms raised to flashing skies
To be just as I should be for now and now forever more
Salt and rain mix upon my cheek and through me the eagle cries

I drove six hours, straight to California. I might have stopped once for gas, but I don't remember it. It was about 11:30 PM when I arrived near their house. I didn't want to barge in on them that late at night, so I parked my truck in the parking lot of a motel. I figured that I wouldn't seem conspicuous, since there must be different vehicles parked there all the time. I had my sleeping bag in the truck with me, and I spread it out along the length of the truck; my legs were between the bucket seats, and my feet were up against the stick shifter. To my amazement, I actually slept pretty soundly. I awoke the next morning to cold, wet windows and a dim, gray light coming through them. It was quiet, except for the sounds of some birds, and it was very cold.

My stomach grumbled. I had small amount of cash with me, so I drove to a nearby fast-food restaurant and got some crappy coffee there. It was enough to start bringing me back to reality, though, and I drank it as I headed toward Mom and Dad's house. I parked my truck and walked up to the door. It was about 8:00AM. I knocked.

The door opened slowly, and Dad stood there in slight shock. He almost couldn't believe his eyes; then he closed the door quickly, and I heard him say to Mom, "Your son is at the front door." Then it was quiet. Mom opened the door a minute later, and they both looked at me as if they were thinking, "What are you doing here?"

"I'm sorry, Mom and Dad," I said, my eyes beginning to swell and tear up again. I must have looked like complete hell. "I am sooooooo sorry that I blamed you for everything. It wasn't your fault! It's all my fault, and I'm so sorry! Please forgive me!" They invited me in, and after some time went by, their anger passed. They had been angry at me for the better part of the past two years, and for good reason. But they forgave me, and I explained the story of Best Path and how messed up things had become. They became truly sympathetic and supportive, and they offered to let me stay with them for a while. But I had to get back to Arizona, to start a new deejay job I had just begun, and I did not want to impose on them. I just wanted to set things right; to apologize; and to tell them how much I loved them, how much I had missed them, and how much they mean to me. They were happy about that, and glad to see that I was finally on the right track. But I did not tell them what my real problem was. That would come about a year or so later. I drove back to Phoenix, but I didn't have anywhere to go, so I spent a lot of time in my truck.

To pass time and help myself, I started reading voraciously, and found a number of books that have been helpful and inspirational in finding myself. One, in particular, is *The Science of Becoming Oneself*, by H. Saraydarian. It is extremely hard to find now, but I was lucky to stumble across a copy at a used book store. I bought it because the title alone seemed fitting, and I was thrilled that I bought it, for it has helped me in amazing ways.

The most profound way the book helped me was through one chapter on detachment. Mr. Saraydarian offered a meditation regimen that focused on detachment from material things. Simply, one sits comfortably and enters a meditative state, then begins to imagine a material item of personal value, which if lost, would cause hurt or anger. These material items could be things such as a car, or computer equipment, nice jewelry, guitars, or whatever else has substantial material meaning. Then, with the image of an item in mind, one would imagine destroying that item, using any method. It could be smashing, burning, crushing, or whatever—the point of the exercise was to desensitize one from the loss of material things. With ownership comes the risk of loss, and many people have serious problems when they lose things they value. I pictured my guitars, among other things, and I am thankful that I did, for a few years later I would realize just how powerful and helpful these meditations would be.

During this time, I also wrote a lot in my journal. This is the first page from that journal.

11 /09/ 98

(Monday) Well! I'm sitting in my truck at the new club in Glendale. Cindy kicked me out of the house, again, Saturday. Saturday night I went to California to speak with my parents. All went well. I've been living in my truck for two nights. I hope to have a job still, at this club. If not, I will go look at other clubs. I was just paged by Cindy at 11AM (a few minutes ago). I will call her back when I get in the club, just to let her know I'm still alive. When I left, I left the impression that I was going to kill myself, but that was just my extreme emotional nature. I'm not going to do that. I'm going to get a grip on my life and live it to be happy, even if that means without Cindy. Best Path is not a happy life and it's not the way I live. I have learned a lot from it and in many ways it has helped me to mature, but it seems to be never ending negatives [this was written before I realized it really was a cult]. *I plan on getting my own place, and a good job, saving money and then possibly moving up to Seattle. Getting out of Arizona would be a good thing to do. I'll ask*

around if anyone needs a roommate. If not, I'll be staying in my truck until I save enough for an apartment. I went to Heartbreaker's last night to talk to the people I know there, and got good energy from some. Positive words are so good to hear. All I've had from anyone else has been negative. I don't need to be told to change by anyone but me, so I'm getting away from that so I can clearly see where I stand with myself and this world.

I've realized that I am a "people-pleaser." I want to make people feel good and I don't want to offend anyone. Club is opening up.

[Later] *Work was slow. I'm sitting alone in my truck behind the Comfort Inn in Mesa. It's about 11PM. I just went to Smith's (grocery) and got some bread and tuna. Saturday Cindy said that I didn't want Anvil when we had him. That is a lie. I've been proud to have my son the entire time. I've never wished I never had him. I love him so much! It's so quiet here.*

About the third night of sleeping in my cold truck, in a motel parking lot, I was trying to settle in to my sleeping bag when I heard some voices outside my truck. I wiped away some of the condensation from the window, and outside, I saw two homeless people walking by. They were wearing rags and looked extremely mangy. One stopped to examine something on the ground, and then they both continued on down the sidewalk.

For the first time in my life, I realized something that I should have known all along, but had to failed to realize, or maybe I did realize it, but it just wasn't something I was consciously aware of. I realized, in that moment, as I was shivering in my truck, my only shelter, that I was no different from them, and they were no different than me. We were all human beings, all made of the same flesh and bone, all of the same earth, all just exactly the same as each other. I was no better than they were and never would be. The core of who we are, of all of us, is the same. We are all human beings; we all suffer; we all feel pain; we all long for love, companionship, friendship, and compassion from others. By the time I had realized all of this, they were long gone. I wanted to run after them to give them a hug, to help them, but I was cold, and my own reality began to sink back in.

Where Are You Now?
You say you love me as you
Push me out the door and
Make me cry again
Our son just sits there
Screamin', "This has to be a dream!"
It's a nightmare
I've got no money
Nowhere to go
Not a friend to call
I'm just sittin'
Waitin' for time to heal my wounds
It's so slow
Where are you now?
And where am I?
I thought we were so close
But we're so far apart!

One of the books I stumbled on at the used book store was called *Recovery from Cults: Help for Victims of Psychological and Spiritual Abuse*, by Michael D. Langone. Its cover jumped out at me as I passed by a small table of books. I bought it and read it in my truck during the following two  days. It was striking how it detailed exactly what was happening in the Best Path group. And it was then that I realized that Best Path truly was a cult. The book is an excellent aid to anyone who has suffered, or is suffering, in a controlling group or cult. It helped open my eyes to the methodologies and reasoning behind why cult leaders behave as they do and how so many people are sucked into their world. Beyond that context, however, the book is excellent for anyone who is dealing with others who are controlling or emotionally manipulative.

I stayed in my truck for a couple more nights before I used a pay phone to call Jim, an old friend from Arizona State, and told him what was going on. I didn't ask him for any favors, but he kindly offered to let me stay at his house for a while. I was more than happy to take him up on the offer and crashed on the floor of his extra bedroom, which was set up as his home office. It was there that I began to get a grip on myself and my life, but there would still be a few more hurdles before I found true happiness within myself. Here is another journal entry that I made after a number of rather dark and depressing entries:

12 /08/ 98

Fuck all that! I'm startin' off new! I WILL BE ME! WHATEVER I AM! Fuck wallowing in whys and bullshit. I'm being me, and having fun doing it.

After I had stayed at Jim's for almost two months, Mom and Dad helped me get into an apartment. Soon after that, I got my job back at a flex circuit company, where I had previously worked in a Computer Aided Drafting position. Sadly, I had quit that job thanks to a suggestion from Rudy and Best Path. It made me feel really good about myself and my situation to get that job back, and it was a bright ray of sunshine in what had become a very dark existence for me over the past few years. As I started to get my head on straight, some more positive turns of events happened.

03 /26/ 99

It's been a while since I wrote in here! I've been back at my CAD/database development job for almost one month. Started March first. It's going GREAT. I managed to get myself into a little debt, "starting over," but now I should be able to pay it off soon. Things with Cindy are better.

Not long after my last writing, she was kicked out of Best Path and she (and I) will never go back. We both see it for what it is, a cult. I'm considering moving back into the house, but having a hard time with the idea. I like my own space. I like to be able to do what I want, when I want, eat and drink what I want. Dress how I want. We're talking about fixing up the house. I suppose I could move back in, but I don't know if I really want to or not.

The next few months were filled with excitement and trepidation as I tried to decide what I was going to do about my gender incongruence. I was enjoying living in my own space for the first time in my life, but it wasn't without its sometimes very dark downs. Being away from Anvil was incredibly heart wrenching, and I missed Cindy intensely, and was feeling like a failure in the family sense. I experimented with my look and began shopping for some new stuff, and I started looking into support groups and counseling. When particular dates came up, like our anniversary, they were the hardest to deal with.

05 /05/ 99
   13 th Anniversary. Last night we agreed that we can't be lovers anymore.
   We will, however, continue to be the best of friends.
   Tonight I want to cut these stupid balls off of me! I hate them.
   Called about electrolysis. Gonna call about counseling, tomorrow.

Even with the positive steps I was taking, life was still very hard at times. With change comes an amazing amount of responsibility, for yourself and for others in your life. You find out that what you thought was a solid given is really just a loose piece of ice, floating around in sea of other loose pieces. You have to work, and work hard, to regain solid footing, to reestablish your whole world. It is tough and trying. There were so many times I thought, "Oh my God, I can't do this!" but I kept on reminding myself that I could do it. It has been said that artists are our own worst critics, but the same is true for everyone—we knock ourselves down all the time, telling ourselves we can't do this or that, or that what we do isn't of value. When you are in the midst of the emotional hurricane that is transition, it is extremely hard to keep your head on straight. That is why it is so vitally important to have support from others who have been through it already. There were so many days when I woke up, folded my hands across my chest, looked upward, and said, "Please, Goddess, help me make the right choices today. Please!" Perhaps she helped me, or perhaps I was speaking to my inner goddess; either way, just saying the words and generating the desire to do the right thing helped me tremendously.

With every two positive steps I took, it seemed as though there would be at least one that would take me back. We have to take the bad with the good, but sometimes things can get so bad. I experienced many high points and many low points, some worse than others, and some that changed my life forever.

A few months after I moved into my apartment, Cindy called, saying she wanted to come over and talk. I agreed, and she came over; with her, she brought a stack of divorce papers. I was surprised that she initiated that, but not overly shocked, even though I did not expect it. Actually, the thought had crossed my mind, but I didn't want us to separate; I wanted us to stay together, even though things were different. In the end, though, I think it was the right thing to do, even though it was so hard and quite depressing. I've heard it said that it takes four years to heal after a divorce. I've also heard it said that it takes as many years as the marriage had lasted. It has been more than four years for us since we divorced, and I think we will never get over it. We will always have a piece of each other, and that is how it should be, I think. You have to take it for what it was worth and move on. That's not so easy when children are involved, but through my experiences, I would have to say that it is absolutely critical that both parents always speak well of one another around their kids. The worst thing one could do is berate the other in their child's presence. I am incredibly thankful to Cindy for speaking kindly about me to others, and I am proud to say that I have always done the same for her.

Something I have found to be important in daily living, for all people, is based on the old saying, "If you don't have something nice to say, don't say anything at all." We really need to practice that, and it is not that hard to do. I think people get into a bad habit of finding fault with and complaining about others, and they get so used to it that it becomes part of their everyday life. I know this is true because I used to do the same thing. It was not because I disliked people; rather, it was because I disliked myself. Being unhappy with who I was gave me a general sense of unhappiness toward others. It wasn't everyone or even anyone in particular. It was mostly just random occasions when others and their actions would bother me. I find now that I don't feel that way at all anymore, and that is because I am happy with who I am. My perspective on other people has shifted one hundred and eighty degrees, and I feel so much more compassion and care for other people now than I ever did before. That is a great feeling! And it is one that I recommend highly. This is, in fact, the core of why I have written this book: when we are in tune within and without, only then we can be in tune with the world. We all have the power to change for the better; we just need to do it for ourselves, and the rest will follow.

Nine Millimeters from the Edge

It has been said that the mortality rate for pre-op transsexuals is approximately 31 –50 percent. That means that one-third to one-half of us makes the conscious decision to take our own lives. I don't think most people understand the ramifications of what this means. I have done a lot of research trying to find specific mortality rates for transsexuals, but this is very elusive data to find. I don't think there is any conclusive data to support those percentages; however, I do know of a few pre-op transsexuals who have succeeded in removing themselves from our lives. I find it very sad that we feel so oppressed by others and by our own feelings that we take this way out of what is ultimately not that bad a situation. Unfortunately, when we are in the throes of depression it is nearly impossible to see our situation as anything but bad. It can take years of struggle, hard work, and determination to find our true self and to find peace in our lives. I must admit, I have had my moments, too, and I came far closer to removing myself from this world than I would like to admit. It is a very scary thing when you come close to death. It is almost unfathomable when you realize how close you came, and that you chose to do it yourself. It's a real eye-opener.

The thing about it is that we feel so hopeless, helpless, and alone. When we first begin to think about it—realize that we really are transsexual—we usually face deep depression because we cannot see any possible way that we could change. We believe we cannot tell anyone else because not only do we often think that we must be insane, but we also believe that others will think we are insane, too. Then we slide into a deep and dark pit of depression and self-loathing, and find it hard to pull ourselves back out. This is one of the scariest, and most dangerous, parts of coping with the transsexual condition. We believe that we are so utterly alone that it won't matter if we are gone. And besides, why keep trying to live a life that isn't our own? The easy way out becomes all too tempting, and some of us finally convince ourselves that death is the only way to solve our problem. Once we do that, our fate hangs in the balance, as we risk everything we know and love to finally find peace.

It is not the way to peace, not the way at all.

Three Out of Four

Empty. Alone. Lost. Dead.
Empty. Alone. Lost. Dead.
Three out of four isn't good enough.
Stick the blade in, let loose the stuff.
Make it four outta four.
Empty. Nothing in me.
Devoid of all emotions except self-hate.
Alone. No one to hold me.
No one to console me when I'm down.
Lost. Knowing nothing.
I don't even know who I am.
Dead. Might as well be.
No one else seems to care.
Slit the vein. Blow the brain.
Break the neck. Choke the lung.
Stab the heart. Rip the throat.
Crash the bike. Take the Big Sleep.
Drown the world away in Mother's womb.
Peace is found at the business end of a gun.

It was cold, black, and heavy in my hands; it had a full, fifteen-round clip inside, with one chambered. It was a nine millimeter semi-automatic pistol with blued finish. The safety was off; the hammer was cocked. I could barely see it through my tears and swollen eyes. To think, this would be the end; a tiny piece of soft metal, blasted from this simple little machine would be what ends all the agonizing, the pain, and emotional turmoil I have endured so long. A simple piece of lead and copper…freedom, peace. I looked up at the window of my apartment and screamed my agony at the world. No one could hear me; there was nothing outside but darkness. It was darkness so thick that it seemed connected with the darkness that shrouded my heart, my head, and my hands. I looked back down at the pistol, beautiful in its simplicity, its only purpose being to take life, or perhaps to save life, in some odd, roundabout way. I was weak from spending what seemed like hours crying and throttling my pillow and punching my mattress, so the weight of the gun seemed even greater in my weakened hands. I was sitting on my knees, on the floor by the foot of my bed.

The tip of the gun felt cold on my temple, which surprised me and started me thinking about other things for a moment. Some might say that over-thinking in a situation could get one in trouble, or may even lead to someone's demise. I must admit, though, that in my case, over-thinking might have actually saved my life! I held the gun to my head—hand shaking; finger on the trigger; chest heaving; heart pounding; mind racing with confusion, desperation, and self-loathing. It wasn't a heavy trigger, quite light actually. All it needed was a gentle squeeze— softer than the effort needed to turn a car key, or to pull open a soda can tab. I looked back at the window through hazy, swollen eyes. The tip of the barrel was warmer now, hardly noticeable. In that moment, it seemed as if my mind and vision had become clear as pure water. I could hear nothing. See nothing. Perhaps it was a rush of adrenaline, knowing I was almost free of my burden, perhaps it was that tunnel they talk about, or maybe just the entrance to it. I sat there, I don't know how long, still as a statue. Staring into…into what? Into something far beyond the space I was in.

A vision opened up before me. It was Anvil, riding his BMX bike, smiling, laughing, and yelling, "Hey, Dad! Watch this!" My eyes were blinded with tears and swelling; my finger twitched. His face was so beautiful, so happy, and so free. "Do a wheelie for me!" I yelled to him. "Okay, Dad!" he yelled back, with a big smile. As he started to ride a wheelie down the driveway, the vision of him faded away and another one faded in. It was me, young, almost his age, with Mom and Dad. We were happy, laughing, being our usual silly selves. It faded away into yet another, Cindy and me, hanging out, laughing, it was the day we had met at the Flagstaff mall. My face contorted, and I burst out a grunt-like cry. The vision faded away, and one more came in to replace it. I was looking at myself, in that moment, from the doorway of my bedroom. I saw myself sitting there, in loneliness and desperation, holding a loaded gun to my own head.

"What are you doing?" I yelled at myself. I turned to see myself standing there, but it wasn't the old me; it was the new me—it was Annah. Her face was alarmed with fear; she held the edges of the doorway as though if she were to let go, Adam would pull the trigger.

"I'm…I…" I mumbled under my pitiful breath. "I don't know!" I screamed as I dropped the gun to my lap and collapsed into a fetal position. I un-cocked the gun and set it far away from myself. Then I stared at the wall in a daze, for I don't know how long, before I fell asleep.

When I woke up, I thought I was waking from a terrible nightmare. But as I looked around, I saw that it was still dark outside, and my gun was still where I had left it. I realized that it was all, indeed, very real. I spent a good amount of time thinking about that moment, about what I had almost done, about how close I came. And I decided that I was not going to have that gun in my possession any more. Sometime, during the next few days, I took it to a gun store and sold it. Anvil went with me. He didn't understand why I wanted to get rid of the gun, of course, because he thought it was cool. He and I had taken it out shooting together in the desert—he with the neat old Winchester Model 67 my dad had given him, and me with my pistol. But I couldn't tell him what I had been through with it that night. He wouldn't understand it at all.

Getting rid of the gun was a symbolic turning point for me. I decided that I was not going to take my own life as a means of avoiding my problems, and getting rid of the gun was a form of commitment in that endeavor. Looking back now, I can only say that I am so glad that I didn't squeeze that tiny little piece of metal, for I would have missed so much beauty and joy in my life.

Part III:
In Tune
Participating in the Symphony of Life

Breaking Down the Walls of Fear

As I began to express myself, in the comfort of my own apartment, I began to realize that just wearing makeup and women's clothing wasn't enough. I needed to figure out who I really was, once and for all. I had already done so much research on the Internet, at the library, and at bookstores that I was sure I was transsexual; with that in mind, I began searching for answers, real answers, about how to deal with my situation. I needed to get out, I needed to connect, and I needed to talk face-to-face with others who were going through, or who had gone through, the same thing.

Integrated
Disconnected. Split in two
Not one, but lost—disarray
One chases one away while the other fights to be free
One hides while the other fights to get the world to see
Frustrated. Lost in me
Not one—disconnected, disarray
Like a dog who is caught in time forever chasing its tail
Exhaustion and desperation reach in to stop this inner ail
Time to bring together
These two that seem to not be one
Time to bring together
And live, live, live now as one
Integrated. Combined as one
Not two, not lost—integration
One embraces the other as they work in congruence
No more hiding in my own bad influence
Strength is to stand together as one
Weakness is divide and conquer
Nations fall that do not stand together
Why can this not be true for me?
Why should I destroy myself because I fear this in me?
Why should I let fear keep me down?
There is no more why, there only is.

Embrace diversity
Stand proud
Unique
Strong and courageous
Never falter
Never question
Never fear your own self
Embrace change
Embrace self
Embrace each other
Discover...
...integration

When I first started out, I had no idea where to start looking for help. At the time, there was no information on the Internet about trans groups in my local area, except for the local Tri-Ess, which is a support group for cross-dressers. I called them, spoke to the director, who's femme name was ironically Cindy, and asked if they helped transsexuals. She said that they did not, but that I should start there, "just in case I wasn't really transsexual." I must admit, I took offense to that statement because I felt that I already knew where I stood. I never did go to a Tri-Ess meeting.

I had heard, or read, about a drag bar downtown called the 307. It was a well-known club, a good place to catch a drag show, and a popular place for gay and trans people to hang out. I don't even remember how I heard about it. I had driven past it a  few times and thought about going in, but never did have the courage. At those times when I was driving over there, I was not dressed *en femme*. I was having a rough time with that, with dressing and going out. In fact, every time I tried to do it, every time I got to my front door and thought I was totally ready to walk through it, I would open the door and be met with a wall of fear so thick that I could not even go through it! There were many nights when I stood there, looking through the crack in my door, smelling the air of the outside world—wishing I had the courage to step outside, walk to my car and just drive somewhere, anywhere, but I couldn't do it.

After many days and nights of frustration, and knowing that counseling was the next step I needed to take, I decided to take a look in the phone book. I thumbed through the Yellow Pages looking for help; I looked through the psychologists' section and was shocked to find one psychologist, Dr. Dickson, who had a small ad that actually included the word *transgender* in it! I got butterflies and called her immediately. I spoke with her assistant and booked my first appointment. I jumped for joy after I hung up the phone, surprised at my own excitement. Just taking a small step toward personal freedom was completely enlightening—I hadn't realized how liberating it would feel.

The day finally came, and I drove up to north Phoenix for my appointment. When I went to Dr. Dickson's office, I went "drab" as they say, not *en femme*. Her office was nice and relaxing, and she

was kind and understanding; she let me talk, a lot. It was scary and exciting at the same time to get all those feelings out, and she was so helpful in listening and talking with me. After my second appointment with her, she gave me information about a local support group, Transgender Harmony, which had an upcoming meeting. She highly recommended that I go, and I was very excited about the possibility.

I went to the meeting,

about a week later, and met the woman who would be my main psychologist from then on, Dr. Christine Grubb. She was, and is, an awesome counselor and person: kind, understanding, gentle, compassionate, and very knowledgeable. At the time, she already had many years of experience working with transsexuals and transgender clients, which made me feel very comfortable.

The night finally came when I got dressed and hoped that I looked good enough to just pass. I was determined to walk through that doorway, to conquer that wall of fear forever. I got my purse, had my keys in my hand, opened the door, stepped out, locked the door behind me, walked to my car, got in, and sat for a minute. I had made it to my car! I took a deep breath, hoping that I would make it to the meeting without being pulled over by a cop. I started my car and headed to my very first support group meeting.

When I arrived, I immediately felt an atmosphere of acceptance and genuine compassion. I was treated with respect and even admiration, which completely blew my mind. In the span of a few hours, I had made twenty, brand-new friends, all of whom understood me better than anyone else ever had before! We discussed issues relating to cross-dressing and transsexualism, as well as other things. After the meeting, I was asked if I would like to go to a "popular night spot." I asked which one that was and was told, "Why, the 307, of course!" I said, "Oh yes! I have been wanting to go there for months! I'm in!"

After the meeting, with my heart beating faster and my mind racing, I followed my new friends to the 307, where I was met with awe and appreciation, and told how beautiful and pretty I was. I laughed it off, thinking they were just saying that to be nice, but they were sincere. "They" were the men, women, and other trans people there. I even got hit on by a very hunky man who looked as if he should have been on the cover of *GQ*! He nearly begged me to go home with him, but since it was the very first time I had ever been out and because I knew he was turned on because I was still pre-op. I was quite grossed-out by the thought, and I did not think it was the right thing to do. I had to say no, thank you, at least a dozen times before he finally left me alone. Despite his persistence and his not taking no for an answer so many times, it sure felt good to be wanted as myself.

In the early hours of the morning, I joined a few of my new friends at Jerry's Restaurant, which fast became our new place to hang out after hitting the clubs.

That night changed my life. It was a magical time, another turning point in my life. That night, Annah Moore was truly born…for the first time! And there would be many more to come!

After that, it was a whirlwind of exciting experiences and personal growth. I began electrolysis, laser treatments, hormones, and with support from the community, I began going out, a lot. I made many new and close friends, one of whom is my dear friend and "older sister," Donna Rose.

Donna and I met at Arizona Electrolysis, where we were both going for hair removal. Late one night, she and I were the only customers in the place. She was at the end of an eight- or nine-hour session (yes, really!), and I was halfway through a three-hour one. Donna and Maria, the owner of Arizona Electrolysis, had decided to order a pizza or two and had asked Angie, my electrolysist, if she and I wanted some, too. We were starving and said we did want some. A half hour later, when the pizza arrived, I heard someone say, "Come on in and get some." I went into another small studio, where the pizza boxes sat on one of the beds. Donna was standing there with a big, droopy pizza slice in her hand, munching away. Her face was swollen and red, and she was cute as a button. I could only laugh because I could so feel her pain!

We stood there and enjoyed pizza together for a few minutes as we introduced ourselves to each other, and then we went back to our sessions. After my session, my face felt just like one of those slices of pizza. On my drives home from the sessions during the winter months, I used to hold my metal Club steering wheel lock against my face. The cold metal felt so soothing on my burning cheeks. The twenty-seven hours of facial electrolysis was well worth it, though.

A few weeks later, Donna and I met again at a big meeting in Phoenix, one at which Dana Rivers came to speak. Dana's story made national headlines when, as David, she lost her job at Central High School in Sacramento, California, after announcing plans to become Dana. She had taken her story on the road and was holding speaking engagements across the country in support of transgender rights. There were a lot of people there, and it was probably only the second or third time I had actually gone out in public as a woman. When I first met Donna, she had seen me as a very androgynous person, so she was slightly shocked when I walked up to her, said hello, and told her who I was. I was wearing a long dark wig, rather than my short blond hair, and was dressed very femininely. What a great night it was. We talked a lot, started to get to know each other, and exchanged phone numbers.

Donna has been an inspiration to me during this whole process. She has always been so positive and full of an energy that is simply contagious. And even when I was going through some of my worst moments, she was there for me and helped me. She is the epitome of a true friend. What I am most proud of her for is her intense dedication to helping others. She's a true jet-setter, traveling around the country, almost weekly, visiting companies to talk about gender rights, and appearing at an infinite variety of meetings and events. If there were a picture next to the word *determination* in the dictionary, it would be one of Donna. I really can't thank her enough for all the great things she has done—for me and for others.

Telling

It is tough enough accepting that you are struggling with the transsexual condition. We deal with this situation our entire lives, and for some of us, it takes a few decades, or more, to finally accept it and move forward to fix the problem. Once I accepted it and began doing something about it, it became time to tell some people, including my parents. I had not told them yet because I had already put them through a lot with the cult-inspired accusations, but I could feel that the time to tell them was drawing nearer.

Dad was driving from California through Phoenix on his way north to attend the funeral of one of his long-time friends, Fred Summer. Fred had been an amazing photographer and was a dear friend of Dad's. I remember Fred from my youngest years; he was a sweet man, who produced incredible pictures. Dad wanted to swing by my apartment and say hello on his way through town, and I was happy about that idea. I thought about telling him, but I knew he already had a lot on his mind, what with the funeral and all, so I put it off. I was feeling a strong need to tell him, though. We talked a bit, hung out some, and decided that I should go along, too. We made the two-hour drive north, stayed with old friends, did a bit of hiking around, and went to the funeral. We came back to Phoenix the following day, and I pondered about telling him. It wasn't until later that day that I finally did tell him, and much to my surprise, he was okay with it.

"Does this mean you're gay?" he asked me. I laughed.

"No, Dad," I said. "It doesn't mean I'm gay. But then, it depends on how you look at it. If I had a male gender identity and body, and I liked men, then I'd be gay. But I have a female gender identity, and I like men, so I am a heterosexual female, for the most part. If that makes any sense!"

We talked about it for a while, and he was completely okay with it, much to my relief. He asked me if it was okay if he told Mom, and I said that I would rather tell her, but I guessed it would be okay. He asked me how far I wanted to go with changing, and I said, "As far as I have to, which is probably all the way."

Dad headed home shortly after that, and he told Mom the

news. She must not have been very thrilled, because for several months after that I would call the house and Dad would answer. I would talk to him some, and then ask if Mom were there and could I speak to her. "She's busy right now," he'd say. It became a regular thing, and it didn't take me long to realize that she didn't want to talk to me. I told him I knew that was what was going on, and he said she just needed time to adjust. "Well, how is she going to 'adjust' if she never talks to me?" I asked. He didn't have much of an answer.

As it turned out, Mom was having an incredibly hard time with the idea of her son becoming her daughter. It wasn't until tragedy struck our family that her perspective on me changed. My cousin, Malisa, a gorgeous young woman who was in her first years of college and doing incredibly well in life, was run over and killed by a reckless driver. This was an incredibly horrible situation for our entire family, and we all grieved very deeply. Time passed, and as I learned later, Mom talked to her brother about his loss and his situation, and also about the struggles she was having dealing with me and the changes upon which I was embarking. She felt as though her son were dying, which in some ways he was, and she just could not accept her new daughter. It was only after my uncle told her that at least she could still wrap her arms around her child and tell her that she loves her that she finally found a way to accept me. She called me not long after that conversation and told me how much she loved me, no matter what.

During this time, I still worked as a database and Web developer at the flex circuit company. I had already been there about a year or so and had discussed my upcoming transition with the company's human resource director, Shirley, who was very supportive and excited for me. She was very helpful, but I did all the work when it came to writing the e-mail to all seven hundred or so of my coworkers. I had already been on hormone replacement therapy, or HRT, for several months and had the appointment for my name change set, which was to take place in August of 2000. I sent the e-mail out to everyone telling them of my upcoming changes, which was about a month in advance of my first full-time day of becoming Annah. Most everyone I worked with was cool with what I was doing, but I am sure that none of them understood it. I barely did!

My debut as Annah at work came; I walked through the front doors of the building, with my head held high and with much excitement. I was greeted with genuine approval, smiles, congratulations, and much interest. The funniest thing was when some of the tool and die makers, grubby guys from the shop downstairs, were "looking for someone" upstairs in the IT department. They just "happened" to walk by my cubicle looking for "so-and-so," just to get a look at the new woman. When the second one came by, I realized their game. I had never seen those guys upstairs before. I had to laugh. One guy came by and asked the same question, to which I said, "Hey now, if you want to come check me out, that's okay; just come on up and talk to me. You don't have to beat around the bush." His face turned beet red, and he smiled and said, "Uh, okay. Sorry." He turned and left. It was quite entertaining, to say the least.

What was perhaps the best part of that experience was that so many people told me that I seemed so much happier and natural, and that being a girl just seemed "so right" for me. I could not have agreed more, but there were still some struggles I faced, and unfortunately I had to make changes, yet again, in front of all those people.

Self-Perception

Self-perception is an interesting thing. Even though I am post-transition, postop, and "post-transsexual", I still see the old "guy me" in the mirror sometimes. It's not that I actually see the old me as much as I know "he" was there, if that makes any sense. It is something of a residual image, I guess. But gladly, as each day, week, and month passes, I see less and less of that old me. We are who we are, and even though we change who we are to a large degree, we are still the same person underneath it all, albeit better than before, if we're lucky. Still, there continues to exist a "phantom" of who we were, if not in reality, then at least in our minds. Interestingly, this phantom former self also lives on through the mail we get in the old name, which seems to never end. Junk mail, especially, just keeps on coming. You'd think they would figure out that people don't exist anymore. It makes me wonder how much junk mail goes out to people who have passed on.

For those of us who are doing the transitioning, we see the tiniest changes day by day, so they are not as evident to us as they would be to others who don't see us for days, weeks, months, or even years at a time. As we evolve into our "new us," the evolution of our appearance is so slow that we hardly notice it. Those who have facial surgery probably do not fall into this category, so they might not see the old them in the mirror as much as those of us who've had no facial surgery. It's somewhat nerve-racking looking in the mirror and seeing the old me still. Granted, it doesn't happen very often any more, and becomes less and less over time. Often, when I am doing my daily routine, like at work for example, and not looking at my own reflection, I have moments where I feel as if my body and my image haven't changed at all. I feel as if the only thing that's really different is that there's no more incongruence to deal with. This is a very strange thing to go through for a number of reasons. First, it makes me feel as if I haven't really come as far as I think I have. But in fact, I have come a long way. Also, it brings up the subtle fears that others might see the old guy, and that I might somehow be "read" as having once been male. Comfortingly, however, this has never happened…or at least no one has ever said anything or asked me if I'm trans or whatever.

There is definitely a link between self-perception and insecurity. We all want to pass, blend in, and live without worrying about what people think of us. It is tough to step into the world during the first phases of transition—when you haven't quite mastered body movement or posture, or your voice is not quite right, or you haven't completed hair-removal, or you feel unsure about any number of other new things you need to be able to do. This is one of the most stressful times during the evolution of our selves, as we take on the challenge of our incongruence. Sometimes this is so uncomfortable, so scary, that we actually question whether or not it was the right thing to do. Our desire for comfort and security cranks up, and we actually consider the inconsiderable: de-transition.

De-transition is actually quite common, and some have said that it is so common that it is almost expected to happen. I don't know if there has been a survey done, but from what I have learned over the years, I would say that nearly 50 percent of the transsexuals I have met have chosen to de-transition for some time before finally going back to and completing transition. During my first transition, which lasted for about five months, I had not yet completed hair removal; the hair on my head wasn't long again yet, and I was still crackly voiced and struggling to get comfortable in public in my new role. The people I worked with at that time told me I looked great; they thought I was totally natural; they said that the changes were absolutely right on and gave me their support. That was all well and good, but my confidence was still screwed up, mainly from the strong, lingering self-perception I described previously. Additionally, being without my family, especially on holidays, caused me incredible amounts of stress and worry, so much so that I ditched my transition and went back to the "old me." The last time my friends in the Phoenix transgender community would see me, for an entire year, would be at the TG Harmony Christmas party in 2000. I went to the party and had fun. With the gift giving and the feeling of family and friends, however, the sadness I felt for being without Cindy and Anvil grew substantially. I hit some excruciating lows, faced bitter depression, and my sense of self-worth plummeted. Just a few days after that party, after deciding to try to be Adam again, I flushed all my hormones down the toilet.

I woke up at about 9 AM. The large house was quiet; my roommate was out of town. It was the tail end of December 2000. The holidays were in full swing, and I had at least a week off from work.

The hazy remnants of sleep left my head slowly. I rolled around in my bed, staring at the cottage cheese-like paint on the ceiling, waiting for it to fall. It never did. Pigeons cooed outside my second-floor window. I hated those pigeons. They always cooed in the morning and woke me when I didn't want to wake. I sat up, grabbed the squirt bottle I had by the window for just such occasions, stuck my arm out the window, and blasted several blasts of water at them. They fluttered off into the blanched Chandler, Arizona, morning sky.

I flopped back down on my bed, buried my head in my pillow, and continued the cry I had started the night before—the cry that had helped me escape the waking nightmare I was living and escape into the peacefulness of dreamland as the warm arms of sleep wrapped themselves around me.

Thoughts of Cindy and Anvil flitted through my mind. Smiling. Laughing. Running around the yard of our house. Being completely silly, and loving each other and our life together. My chest wrenched as if a large cargo strap had been cinched around it. I lost my breath. My heart seemed to stop. My pillow became the recipient of a number of agonizing screams of pain, frustration, anger, and utter helplessness. I rolled around my bed and screaming into my pillow, wishing I would just die.

A little while later I got up and stumbled to the bathroom to relieve myself. Better there than in my bed, I thought. It was bad enough to feel like complete crap, and I had no desire to clean up after my miserable self. As I walked into the bathroom, I grabbed the sink edge with my left hand and the towel hanging on the wall with my right. I turned my swollen, bloodshot eyes to the mirror— big mistake. I hated what I saw. In that mirror was the face of everything in my entire life that I loathed. I screamed at it. I punched it—thankfully not hard enough to break the mirror, or my hand. I fell to the floor, a crumpled mess of a human being. Desperate. Alone. Depressed. Hopeless. And so utterly afraid.

I don't know how long I stayed there. Even though I had again tried to figure out how to take the "easy way out", I knew I couldn't kill myself, and after realizing it yet again, I decided that I would do anything to be with Anvil and Cindy…even if that meant stopping the process of changing my body.

With renewed determination to suppress it all, and in desperation to live the life I wanted so much to have, and felt so obligated to, I opened the medicine cabinet and took my bottle of estrogen pills from it, popped the top off them, and poured them into the toilet. With a miserable "fuck you" and a quick pressing of the toilet handle, Annah went swirling down into oblivion.

My face was still swollen. My eyes were bloodshot and red. I put on my jeans, my black leather boots, a t-shirt, and the black leather biker jacket Cindy had given me years before. I didn't look exactly the way I had before, but close enough. I got my keys, got in my car, and headed back to Cindy's house.

I pulled into the driveway, not knowing what I was going to do, unsure if what I was doing was right. I began to cry again, but forced it away with a pseudo-macho fistful of repression. I opened my car door, stepped out, and walked to the house. Since I was still welcome there, I walked on in. Cindy was standing at the kitchen sink. I stopped in the living room and stared at her. I loved her so much, and I was so happy that we would be together again. I had missed her so much. She turned, slowly, as if it was all a dream.

"Adam?" She said with disbelief.

"Yeah, babe, it's me." I stood tall, smiled, walked toward her, and stretched out my arms.

"Really?" She asked, her face contorting with a mixture of relief, confusion, and worry, "Are you really back?"

"Yes." I said, and we hugged tighter than ever before.

That year, I bought a brand new street bike, a Yamaha V-Star 1100. I loved that bike. It was, as I called it, a "Hardly Davidson," but it was low to the ground, fast, loud, and very masculine.

That bike seemed to symbolize a lot during that year, and perhaps during my life. I got it for a few reasons: I love to ride, and it was very masculine—black and chrome, loud, and tough. I cut my hair really short, got a black helmet, and the works. It felt good—like old times, comfortable, like being back in the old saddle that had been broken in twenty years ago. Still, the inner turmoil stirred, however subtly. I tried to push it down, to keep it at bay, but it was not possible, and it affected my every waking moment, and most of my sleeping ones, too.

Part of going back to the old me entailed having to tell all my co-workers that I was going back. This was embarrassing, to say the least, but I was very determined to do it. I sent out this e-mail to all the employees:

Dear Friends and Coworkers,

First of all I would like to thank you for the kindness and compassion you have shown me during the past six months. I've been through a lot during this time and without your kindness and support I would not have been able to do what I have done.

I do not wish to cause further confusion for you, and I'm sure that to you it must look like I am a rather confused character, but sometimes a person has to walk so far down a path before they know for sure whether-or-not that path is the correct one for them to follow and call their own. As you know I've been dealing with the issue of Gender Dysphoria all my life and it was apparent to me several months ago that the proper path for me was to change my body to match my mind. But in doing so, that choice brought insurmountable consequences and losses that I can no longer bear. My family is the main thing I am referring to. My spouse, my son. Both of whom could not understand my decision to make these changes, but who supported me nonetheless. Both of whom have wished for me to be the person I was before. Both of whom have been patient and strong and graciously giving in their love and devotion to me, no matter what. But still, choosing to change my sex was choosing to leave my family behind. That is a price, I have learned, that I cannot pay.

Along with that there are many other reasons I wish to return to the "old me". But know that I can never return to who I was before, because I've traveled a path of self-exploration and learning which has taught me more than I could have ever known about myself had I not done so. Those reasons shall remain mine and mine alone. It is not necessary to tell the world why we choose to do what we do, but I do feel that when we make such major changes in our lives, such as this, that those we are close to, and those we work with, should be given the courtesy of knowing some of the reasons why we are doing things.

With that said, I would like to tell you that I will not be pursuing the physical changes that I had intended to when I began this journey. I am changing my name back to Adam, and I will live the rest of my days as the person I should have been all along.

Thank you for your support. I know it's hard to understand, but I thank you for your attempts to understand and your kindness and compassion.

Sincerely,

Adam Moore

Ouch. That is very hard for me to read now! My coworkers did not react very much, toward me, at least. A few said they were happy for me no matter what, and one guy was happy that he could call me "dude" again. Overall, everyone except for one young engineer, took it in stride and treated me well. That one engineer never said anything verbal to me or about me, as far as I know, but the way he looked at me with his stupid grin said it all. I thought it was very strange how he did that, even months later, but to each his own. It is his way of expressing his discomfort with his own inability to understand a situation. Would be interesting to see how people like him would deal with the transsexual condition. But I would never wish it on anyone, that's for sure.

Picking Up the Pieces

What Was There
It's been so long since the rain ended
I've had such a hard time seeing through the gray
But now I put the past behind me
The new Reign begins today
Thrive on the now. Relinquish yesterday
It's time for a new reality
Purge the clouds from the soul
Grasp hold of self-control
What I thought was destiny was just a detour
My mind is clear and I see what was there all along.

For nearly one year, Cindy and I tried to make it work. I had cut my hair short and trying my best to be a man again. The first few months seemed okay. The sex was okay at first. The intimacy was incredible. But as the days and weeks went by, we both slipped back into the realization that things between us would never be the same again. I became depressed. I wasn't a man, and I knew I couldn't pretend to be one anymore. I couldn't try to be the aggressor during sex, so I stopped trying at all. I became increasingly depressed, and Cindy suggested that we just admit that we shouldn't be a couple anymore, so we stopped trying.

That year was not an easy one, but in the grand scheme of things, I think it was a necessary one. Trying to be the old me was obviously not working very well, and Cindy, especially, could see it.

In fact, it was she who suggested that I get back on the track of following my heart and finding my true self once and for all. These were bittersweet words that opened up the still-fresh gashes in my heart, and at the same time they comforted and soothed my whole being with relief.

There were two very strong forces working within me during that year. The first one was my intense desire to keep our family alive and to live up to the expectations everyone had for me. I didn't want to let anyone down, especially Cindy and Anvil.

Another force, though, was working within me and was the one that knew the truth. Deep inside, I knew what I needed to do; perhaps going back was a way to prove to myself, and to everyone else, that changing was the right thing for me to do after all. In the end, I am glad I took that year to double check, to make sure of things. I had a few very dark bouts of depression, but I ended up making it through them without incident. Again, I found that turning to music was one of the best recourses for dealing with my feelings and frustrations.

Several years had passed and a lot had happened since Craig's death and Thunderin' Reign's demise. My awesome IT job came to an end in mid-2001, when the company was bought out and the location I worked in was shut down. They did offer me the position of Webmaster for the company, but we would have had to move to Minnesota, and that was just out of the question. The saving grace was a very healthy severance package; I invested part of it into recording equipment, and spent another part on Lasik eye surgery for Cindy. The rest went to savings. After getting some recording gear together, and getting a new Marshall guitar amp and a killer new Jackson Randy Rhoads RR1 (Flying V), Cindy and I began to write some songs. They were pretty heavy, both musically and emotionally. She poured her heart and feelings out about all my gender-related stuff and how she was affected by it, and I can't blame her for doing that, even though it was very hard for me to have to hear it over and over again. After a few months of practicing on our own, we named the band Bittersweet and decided it was time to get ourselves a drummer and a bass player.

We auditioned a few drummers, and had a girl playing drums with us for a couple of weeks before we decided she wasn't the right one. We checked around again and found a good player, Steve, who was a cool guy. He learned the songs quickly; we wrote some stuff together, and not long after that, we began looking for a bass player. That was a position that was not easy to fill; in fact, we never did find the right one, and the band remained the three of us: Cindy, Steve, and me. I had restarted HRT and was in the process of changing my name back to Annah again. I was getting ready to transition for the second, and last, time. I decided that Steve probably needed to know about all this, although I'm not sure why. I talked to Cindy about it, and then let him know. He seemed cool about it, and that was that; after a few weeks went by, however, he started showing little interest in what we were doing, saying that he wanted to do something heavier. The band just crumbled; we mutually decided that things weren't working out, so we parted ways.

Cindy and I had been living together in the house that year, and even after I started hormones and began living more and more of my life in female mode, I lived there. The three of us tried to live together and make things work as a family, but there was another underlying current running through the energy that existed between Cindy and me—it was the fact that she was not comfortable with what I was doing, coupled with the fact that I knew she wasn't. It caused a serious rift to develop, which became more and more unbearable as the days passed. She coached Anvil's soccer team, and I hung out with them sometimes, in drab. No one there knew about me, about us, about all that turmoil. But it was so close to the surface for me and becoming harder and harder to contain.

Unbeknownst to me, Cindy was having a much harder time dealing with my changes than I thought. I had been going to weekly meetings, where any number of other transgender and transsexuals from the community would meet for coffee. We had fun hanging out and being social, spreading our transgender wings, as it were. One evening, I went to one of the meetings. Cindy had seemed okay with it when I left, but when I got home, it was apparent that she was having a much harder time of it than I had known. Since she never was one to lash out or go into fits of rage or anything like that, but what happened this particular night made a big statement.

I pulled my car into the driveway, and as I did, I noticed there were things strewn about the ground. At first I thought they were some of Anvil's toys, or the neighbor's kids' toys, but the closer I got, the more clearly in view the things became, and the more knotted my stomach became, too. I parked at the end of the driveway and stepped out of my car, almost in disbelief. One of the electric guitars I had designed myself, and built completely from scratch, was smashed to pieces all over the driveway. There were chunks here and there; the strings still connected the bridge to the headstock, but the neck and fretboard were gone. It was a complete loss.

I picked up one of the pieces of the fretboard, the one with a pearl inlay of an eye that I had spent a day making, and thought about Cindy and the immense amount of emotion that she had unleashed on it. I found it interesting that I wasn't mad; in fact, my own emotions were as cool as could be, and that surprised me. Then I remembered the detachment meditations and understood immediately just how valuable they had become. I was not letting anger, rage, or sadness take me over; I was thinking about Cindy, about her pain, and hoping that she was okay. I just wanted to make sure she was all right.

Inside the house, I found her slouched down in the sofa, arms crossed, and a very pissed-off look on her face. I asked her if she were okay; then asked her why she had shattered the guitar.

"You took something that I loved away from me!" she said, pain and anger in her voice and face. "So it was only fair that I take something you love away from you!"

"There's a big difference between a guitar and…" I started, and then stopped myself. "I'm so sorry, Cindy." I didn't know what to do. There was nothing I could say to help ease her pain; hell, I was the one causing her pain! So I walked back outside to pick up the pieces. As I looked around the yard for more guitar bits, I saw that my makeup and jewelry box was broken and lying on the front lawn. My jewelry was strewn all over the dry, hay-like grass, and the front bedroom window was broken. My heart sank. This wasn't what I wanted for either of us, especially for her. I loved her so much, so deeply, and I wanted only the best for her. I felt so lost. I sat there, picking my earrings out of the grass, and cried.

A little while later, Cindy came outside, squatted next to me, and helped me pick up my things. We looked in each other's eyes;

the pain seemed to form beams of energy from one of us to the other. She was sorry and so was I. We didn't know what to do but take one moment at a time, and hope for the best out of a dire situation.

During that rough time, I needed a break from everything. I couldn't find work, and I was growing emotionally weary from trying to live in the house with Cindy. My relationship with Anvil had been awesome, as it always has been. For that I am incredibly thankful. It's amazing, but throughout this whole experience, he is the one person who has seemed the least fazed by what I went through. He just rolled with the changes and was a happy camper. Thank goodness for him; he's a blessing.

To get a break, I took a trip to Austin to visit Donna for a few days. I flew out there, and was Annah the whole time! It was a great experience in so many ways. Donna took me down to 6th Street, which blew my mind and made me realize just how crappy Phoenix was in terms of a music scene, or lack thereof, and opportunities for musicians. I fell in love with Austin immediately, and I enjoyed my time there while it lasted, which seemed all too brief. Donna told me that if I ever needed a place to stay, I was welcome to live with her until I got my situation worked out. It would not be very long before I took her up on that offer, and although I didn't realize it at the time, my intentions for myself and my life had already changed forever.

I returned to Phoenix refreshed, but with a bit of trepidation. The days passed, and I took care of the things I needed to take care of, such as getting my name changed to Annah once and for all, and getting my new Social Security card and driver's license. It's funny, but it was actually harder to get an *M* put back on my license when I went back to being Adam for that year! I was required to take my birth certificate down there to prove I had been born male. They just didn't believe I was not female, which, in retrospect, was awesome! Since I had my letter of recommendation from Dr. Grubb, getting the letter *F* put back on my license went very smoothly.

Cindy and I tried to live together still, but it was hard. I was pondering my options. Should I get my own place? I had no job. Should I move to Austin? I didn't know what to do about all that, so I just kept on keeping on, taking my HRT each day, going to weekly meetings at the coffee shop, and supporting Anvil in his endeavors, all the while assuring myself that things would work out for the best.

In the end, there is nothing wrong with de-transitioning and going back for a while, or for good, if that's what is truly right for the individual. The entire experience of changing sex and gender is a test of who we are, to the very core of our identities. Gender is an infinite spectrum, from ultra-masculine to ultra-feminine and every shade of the rainbow in between. As people who have internalized their need to live on the feminine end of the spectrum but who have lived on the masculine end, we have a lot of things to experience before we figure out exactly where we fit in. Often, because we have forced ourselves into the most masculine end of things, we have no real idea where on the spectrum of gender we really belong, and we are used to doing gender-related things in extreme and often stereotypical ways. Unfortunately, our world is predominantly bi-gendered and society doesn't yet understand that there is every shade of gender and sexuality in between. This contributes greatly to why we often go ultra-*femme*.

Something that appears to be a common factor in both transitioning and de-transitioning is what I call the "slingshot effect." What commonly happens with most transsexual women, until we accept our situation and begin to change, is we usually over-masculinize our lives. This is mostly a psychological wall we build to protect ourselves from others finding out about us, and it aids in repression, too. As we begin to experiment with the feminine side of life in our early transitional phase, we have a tendency to over-do it and go to the extreme of the *femme* scale. This can cause us to appear somewhat freakish to others, especially if we haven't erased all the traces of masculinity yet.

Often, we go so far to the feminine side of the gender spectrum that we freak ourselves out, and we sling shot back to the masculine side because it's our comfort zone. We know what to expect there; it's where we felt safe for so many years, and our loved ones are usually quite thrilled to have the old us back in their lives.

Although many transsexuals experience this, there are other trans people who don't experience the slingshot effect. They take it slowly and don't overcompensate on the feminine side of things. Maybe this is because they were already androgynous to begin with. Maybe it is because they are more cautious, or maybe they are just more secure about what they are doing. Or maybe they don't have a spouse and a child to consider.

Turning Points

In early April 2002, Donna came from Austin to visit some friends in Phoenix. She called me up and wanted to know if I'd be interested in joining her and a few old friends for some dinner in Scottsdale. I was happy to accept. I thought about asking Cindy if she would like to come along, but she had always declined when I had invited her to any kind of event or gathering that involved the trans community. So I decided that I wouldn't bother asking her this time; I was sure she wouldn't want to go.

The morning of the dinner, a Saturday, Anvil had a soccer game at a local field, and the three of us went there together, as usual. I was in drab, which was my usual look for the soccer-related events. We took our camping chairs, and I took my camera; we planned on having a nice time, watching our son kick the ball around. But I had a debilitating migraine headache, and Cindy was perturbed. We sat, silently for the most part, watching Anvil play. Cindy broke the silence:

"Why didn't you invite me?" she asked, referring to the dinner.

"I didn't think you'd want to go; that's not your scene," I said, rubbing my temples.

"You could have at least asked me," she said, implying that I should feel guilty.

"You would have said no," I said, getting frustrated. "You never want to go with me where trans people are involved." I folded my arms and watched the kids kick the ball on the bright sunny field. My head was pounding even worse than it had already been. Migraine. Horrible feeling. A few minutes later, I was rubbing my temples as the father of another player walked past us; he looked down at me and said, "Now there's a man with a headache!" I wanted to kick his kneecap off, but I was too dejected to do anything but cringe and start to cry. He just kept walking on by.

I looked at Cindy, who was staring at the field, as if to say, "I know how that must make you feel, but I'm not being sympathetic." I looked at Anvil, who was running around the field, totally carefree. I wanted to crawl into the ground right there and be no more. I got up and figured I would walk the several miles back home alone, but then I realized I couldn't, so I found a quiet spot under a big tree in the farthest corner of the soccer fields. I sat there, with my knees drawn up to my chest and my arms wrapped around them, and I cried heavily. After a while, I made my way back to my chair. Cindy said nothing. We sat silently until the game was over. Then we drove home.

I closed myself up in my room for a few hours; I curled up into a ball on my bed and cried the whole time. Then I remembered that I was having dinner with Donna that night and her words echoed in my mind: "You can always stay with me if you need to; you know that. There's always a place in my home for you." All of a sudden, everything began to fall into place. My path suddenly became very clear.

Sometimes we have these moments that we think we'll never get beyond. We think that they're going to be the end of our existence, but most of the time they become the turning point in our lives. That is what that day on the soccer field was for me. It was the turning point, an epiphany, and the day of reckoning. The simple statement that a man made to me that morning was the proverbial straw that broke the camel's back. It's funny how things work out like that. Changes in perspective and direction of one's life come when you least expect them, and often from places and people you can't even anticipate.

That evening, I drove up to the restaurant in Scottsdale and met up with Donna and friends. We had a nice dinner; we laughed and talked about life, but I was anxious to ask Donna if her offer was still open.

"Is that offer still open?" I asked her.

"Of course, babe!" she said, with her usual bright smile.

"Then I would like to take you up on it, if I may," I said.

"Well, of course!" she said. "When do you want to move out? A couple of months?"

"Two weeks?" I said, with a blend of a question and a statement. She was surprised but said it was not a problem at all. We talked lightly about the logistics, and then enjoyed the rest of the evening with the others. As I left the restaurant, my heart began to race with excitement and a little fear. Was I really going to do this? Could I? Could I just pack up and leave like that, so all of a sudden? Well, it wasn't all of a sudden to me, but it would probably be that way for Cindy and especially to Anvil. Oh my God, I was facing some massive fears, but my resolve and determination were strong, and my desire to find myself, or die trying, was too strong to waver.

When I got home, I began organizing a few of my things. Cindy asked me what I was doing, and I told her I was packing some stuff, and that I was going to move to Austin. She was shocked. I explained to her how I knew that she couldn't bear to watch the "man" she loved so much go through the changes I was going through, and that I didn't want to force her to have to deal with that. It wasn't fair to her, or to me, and especially not to Anvil. Anvil had never once had any problems with me changing, or changing back. He had always just rolled with it. What a trooper! He and I have always had an amazing bond of honesty and sharing that we both cherish and respect, and my respect for him as a person, throughout his whole life, has enabled him to trust me implicitly. I value that above all, I think.

Later that night, I told him I had to move away and why. We cried a lot. It was very hard, but not as hard as the final moments when I was pulling my car out of the driveway. I had packed everything I thought I would need into my car: my guitars, my amp, my computer, my clothes, and my personal stuff, all the necessities. The car was packed to capacity.

On the morning of April 24, 2002, a bright, sunny day in Phoenix, Arizona, we hugged each other and said our good-byes, and the two of them stood together at the front of the house, Anvil's arms wrapped around Cindy's waist. Our eyes were swollen and red; our faces were wet with tears. That was the last picture I have in my memory of living there with them; it was the last time the three of us would live together as a family, and it wrenched my heart so forcefully that I thought I was going to die before I got out of the driveway. I cried for the next few hours, as I left the old me behind and drove toward the person I was meant to be.

I drove sixteen and a half hours straight to Austin and arrived at Donna's house at about midnight that night, after having stopped a couple of times for gas and fast food. I was exhausted, but I was happy to be there. She got up to greet me, opened her house to me, and then went back to bed. I unloaded a few items from my car, went to my new room, aimed my useless body at the bed, and crashed hard.

A couple of days later I wrote this song:

Wings of Destiny
Sometimes I wish things could be the way they used to be
But you'll always be the deepest part of me
I hate this too but we know I must be on my way
May seem unclear right now but you will know some day
Why things don't turn out like we wish they would be
Always blinded by the little things but someday we will see
Get yourself together and start to live your life again
No more sorrow stop thinking about all that could have been
We are courageous, proud, we are alive and strong
The separation of our paths will never prove us wrong
Things can turn out just the way that they should be
We have control but our lives still ride the wings of destiny
Now is the future of the past that we once knew
The future now will start to become clear to you
If you burn the bridges of the path you thought you could not go
You'll only lose the chance to make that future known
Life will unfold before you when you set yourself free
You can take the reins and guide the wings of destiny

I spent the next few months doing a lot of mental organization. I didn't really have time for much else, besides trying to find a job. I was still struggling to find a tech job doing Web development or database work, but I couldn't even get a call back, let alone an interview. Ever since I had moved, I had been living fulltime as Annah, finally, and in a town where not one person—except for Donna, and that had been briefly—knew me as Adam. From that moment on, all my new friends and acquaintances would know nothing about the old me, unless I told them, and that's how I wanted it. I just wanted to be myself for once in my life, to enjoy the simple things—to be called Annah, and to be referred to as "her" and "she," the proper pronouns for who I am. I didn't want people asking me about my past or any of my history. I just wanted to find out who I really was and run with it, for the first time in my entire life. Thankfully, that's exactly what I got the chance to do.

One night, I went to a great club down town on Riverside Drive called the Steamboat. Donna's friend, Julie, who was also trans, took me down there to see a local group called Del Castillo. They were a Spanish/flamenco band, with two amazing classical/Spanish/flamenco guitar players, the Del Castillo brothers. Julie and I instantly became friends, and we later enjoyed hanging out together on a number of occasions. Before the Del Castillo show, as we sat in the arena-style seating in front of what is still the biggest "small venue" stage in town, I said to Julie, "I am going to be playing on that stage in six months! Just you wait and see!" I was so excited about the possibility, and I meant it; I was very determined.

It would be about five months later when I actually did play my guitar on that stage.

After a few months of time uselessly spent trying to get a tech job, I started to worry. Then Donna suggested I try Guitar Center. I laughed. "Yeah, right!" I said. She reassured me that I would be perfect for a job there, and so I got an application and turned it in with a resume. With that, and with her excellent reference, they actually did hire me. So my very first job as Annah Moore was at Guitar Center, selling guitars on the guitar floor. I was so busy working and driving that I hardly had the time to realize what was going on, that I was beginning to find myself.

While I was at Guitar Center, I made a lot of connections with musicians, of course. I even found my first Austin band, Boneglove. They took me in as one of two new guitar players. I was honored, and they were impressed that a girl could play guitar the way I did. I had reservations about telling them about myself, but eventually I did, and I'm glad I did. They were very accepting and curious. I told them a lot, and they were genuinely amazed. There were six of us in the band and Ali, who played keys and sang, remained one of my best friends from Austin. She has the voice of an angel, too; you should hear her sing—simply incredible.

After a month or two of working at Guitar Center, I realized just how much I needed my own space, a place of my own, downtown. Donna's house was pretty far north, and I really needed to be in closer proximity to the Austin night life and music scene. I looked around, found a drummer who was looking for a roommate, and moved in to the extra bedroom in his duplex, which he was renting out. It was cheap enough, but he was a smoker, and there were stalactites of smoke particles hanging from the ceiling. My clothes reeked of stale menthol cigarette stench, even though he smoked outside. It was nauseating, and I could only stand it for a few weeks, so I began looking for another place.

The other guitar player in Boneglove offered to let me stay in his apartment until I could get my own place. He was a maintenance man at the complex he lived in, and he had a large, two-bedroom unit that he got for free. He said I could stay there and only pay $100 a month, which to me was absolutely perfect! I took him up on that. It was a good arrangement because we got to play guitars together whenever we had the chance to, but it was tough at times, too. It's often hard living with other people. I have always had a hard time doing it and much prefer to live alone, or with my son. So things didn't work out so well for us; we had a few frustrating moments, but it was all right in the end. I realized I needed my own space, so with his recommendation of an apartment finder friend of his, I found the most kick-ass apartment in Austin! And it was cheap!

Boneglove came and went about a year or so later. It was a good experience while it lasted, although I had to tolerate a good amount of emotional manipulation from the band's leader and bass player. Being told exactly what notes to play, for every bar of every song, and having minimal creative input, became too much, and when Ali quit the band, I followed suit. It felt great to get out of there.

As mentally tough as dealing with the band was, it wasn't so bad for me, because I had already had a lot of experience with emotional manipulation from Rudy and the cult situation. I was hypersensitive to that kind of thing and recognized it in this situation almost immediately. Having "been there, done that," I figured I could handle it, but I was wrong. There is no point in dealing with emotional manipulators. It's just not worth it. The band did do a lot for me, though, in terms of visibility as a guitarist in Austin. People knew the name Boneglove when I mentioned it, and on a Monday night show at the Steamboat, we had ninety-seven people come, just to see us play.

That night, I was on stage, looking out at the crowd and thinking about that night that Julie and I had sat there and I had told her I'd be playing that stage one day. It was an amazing feeling to know that I had actually made that dream come true; it warmed my heart and gave me more hope for the future. That night, one of the most amazing things I have ever heard came from a beautiful woman, who was in the crowd in front of the stage. She was part of a sea of people that had gathered there and were rocking out. Between songs, she caught my attention, and with so much enthusiasm, she screamed out, "You rock! I wish I were you!" It took me a moment to process it and to realize what she had said. I have spent my life seeing women I admired and have thought those same exact words: "I wish I were you." And there, in front of me, was a beautiful woman, screaming those words at me! She had no idea how much that brief moment moved me. It's one of those precious ones, a jewel of time and space that I will always cherish. I wish I had been able to find her, to thank her. Perhaps she'll read this, and she will know just how good it made me feel that night, and will continue to for the rest of my life.

Moving to Austin was not without some excruciating moments when I was alone in my own space. Several times, usually at night, my heart would break at the thought of living without Anvil and missing so much time with him. I cried myself to sleep many nights thinking about that—wondering if I had done the right thing, wondering if I would survive, worried that he might some day resent me for leaving. My hope has always been that he would respect the fact that I did what I had to do to be happy and free, and to overcome my plight. After four years now, I'm pretty sure I won't have to worry any more. When we get together, we have great times, and there is so much love and happiness. He is very well adjusted, considering all that he's been through in his young life, and I have no doubt he'll do great things when he's older.

What Do You Do?

What do you do when you love someone so much it hurts?

What do you do when all you have of them is a picture to look at?

What do you do when you just want to bury your face in their hair and smell the wonderful way they smell…but all you have is their picture?

What if you just want to tell them you love them more than anything or anyone in the world as you hug them and kiss them…but they're two thousand miles away?

What if things had just worked out like we dreamed?

What if…what if…It changes nothing.

Nothing changes. We are forever.

My love for you will never die.

You own the deepest part of me.

I'm not only away to try and save myself,

I'm away in hopes of saving you, too, because you mean so much to me.

I love you.

Harmony Within / Harmony Without

In the concert of nature it is hard to keep in tune with oneself if one is out of tune with everything...
—George Santayana, American poet and philosopher

The retuning of myself did not come easily, or without cost. There is no guidebook for transsexuals. There's no automatic tuner, like the ones I have for my guitars. There are, however, many others like me who have been down the similar road and are gracious enough to help others like us when we need help the most. It is for this reason that I hope to return the favor, to them, in a roundabout way, and to others like us, to family members and friends, and to whomever else, by reaching out in my own ways to lend a hand so that we, and the rest of the world, may take one more step toward being in harmony as a whole.

Overall, mine is a life that is not that much different from anyone else's, but I definitely have had a different perspective than most people and have taken a different path to become myself. Sadly, many folks automatically judge people like me as strange, sick, perverted, insane, or evil, all of which could not be further from reality. For most of my younger years, even I thought all those things about myself, but deep down inside, I knew I was a good person. When a person is born into this world with such a different set of circumstances to face, it either destroys the person or makes the person stronger. I believe that I am very lucky it has not destroyed me, and that ultimately embracing my differences has helped mold me into a decent human being after all. I am proud of who I am and where my path has led me, and I look forward to every bit of the future. That's something I couldn't say several years ago, at least not without fear and shame creeping into my hopes and dreams.

It has taken me many years to finally tune myself up; I did not know why I was so out of tune with life, or more specifically, out of tune with myself. I liken my life to a musical instrument, such as the guitar. A person who has never played guitar before most likely doesn't yet understand how to tune it, play it, or maintain it. Trying to play an out-of-tune guitar can be an extremely frustrating experience, to say the least. Once you realize the problem, that the instrument being out of tune is causing you to be unable to make harmonious music, then you can attempt to set things straight—you start turning the tuning pegs, hoping to get the thing to sound good. You begin experimenting with the various parts of the instrument in often feeble and unsuccessful attempts to correct the nauseating cacophony that the thing emits when you try to play it, and in so doing, you may end up breaking a lot of strings.

A large number of guitar players I have known throughout the past twenty-something years have gone through this, and they have broken many a string trying to tune their first guitars. I have, too. Sometimes it takes practice, intuition, or a good guitar teacher to show you how to tune a guitar, for the particular tuning required by a guitar is unusual. Tuning a guitar is not straight forward, like tuning a violin, or cello. There are two strings that must be compensated one half-step from the other four. Who knows this when they start playing? Not many. The best way to learn how to tune and play a guitar is for someone who knows what he or she is doing show you; you need a teacher. Then your learning and skill development will accelerate at a much faster and much more valuable pace.

There are not very many teachers out there who can tell you that your very being is out of tune. It's not as if we can strum a chord and have everyone in the room tell us something is wrong with us. People cannot look at us, or hear us speak, and say that we are transsexual, at least not at first, when we're not outwardly showing it. I think that it is because we know that people can't tell that we stay locked inside ourselves for so many years, even after we realize why we're out of tune with ourselves. Even when we have realized we are trans, and we try to inform others of our situation, they still do not believe that we are so out of tune with ourselves because they cannot see any visible signs. But once we start to change, once we start tuning ourselves up, changing our bodies to finally match our minds, when they see and hear us, then they finally start to get it.

Both Sides of the Line

Mom once asked me, "Are you sure you want to be a girl?" and I told her that it wasn't a matter of wanting to be a girl; it is just that I am a girl. And while it was tough being a girl in a boy's body, it is often tough being a woman in this society, too, although I am much happier now, even with all the new issues that accompany womanhood. I am simply happy to be myself and to know who I am. Even though I face a different set of problems, they feel like the right problems. They feel like the kinds of problems any woman would face.

One of the most amazing things about my life has to be the fact that I have been one of the lucky few to experience both sides of the gender/sex line. It's not such a cut-and-dried line after all; it's actually somewhat blurry these days, but for the sake of simplicity, let's just go with the common distinction: men and women, male and female.

I can't say that I was ever truly a man because inside I wasn't a man—just outwardly. Yet I did get to experience what it was like to be a man. Though there were some advantages, they were certainly not worth sacrificing who I am. Now I can report that I feel complete and whole as a woman, and I feel like I am experiencing life completely, as a complete person. Granted, I have been living as a woman for only a few years, but I have experienced an amazing amount of social interaction, and the contrast between the two ways of life has been eye opening.

Perhaps one of the most intriguing aspects of crossing the gender/sex line is the fresh perspective it gives one about both sexes. It is more than just perspective; it is the actual experiencing of the two sexes that has been amazing. There are not many people who know what it is like to actually be both sexes, and so, I think that it is one of the most incredible things one can experience in this world that is so rigidly constrained by a bi-gendered social foundation.

Each gender has distinct advantages over the other, if you wish to call them advantages. They are more like unspoken rules of gender engagement. Keep in mind, too, that my experiences are only from American society, and a small portion thereof. But from what

I have read, and from what I have learned from others, it appears to be pretty much the same in most countries.

Before I transitioned I found it frustrating how often I would smile at people who never returned my smiles with anything but looks of "what are you smiling at, jerk?" It was rare for anyone to smile back at me, and it became increasingly frustrating. I began to think that the world was full of a bunch of jerks that didn't care about anyone but themselves. But looking back on it, I think there was far more to it than that. There were certain ways of being treated as a man that I did not recognize until after I crossed the gender line, and my perspective changed.

After transition, one of the first things I noticed when I started to go out in public was that people actually returned my smiles—and they often smiled at me first. This totally blew my mind, and I began to wonder about the reason behind such a drastic change. I figured it could be one thing, or a combination of different things. Maybe they didn't feel threatened by me? Maybe they didn't feel confused by my appearance? Maybe there was a subconscious energy around me that they picked up on—perhaps the energy I had exuded before was dark and confused, and now it was bright and uplifting. Maybe I was just walking around with a smile on my face all the time. It was hard to tell, but I didn't care; all I knew was that it felt great to be smiled at for a change.

It seemed like after transition, people in general actually opened up to me more. I am not sure if this was because people are more apt to be more open with women, or if it was because I seemed more approachable. It is probably a combination of both. It is really interesting how men and women treat each other differently. As a woman, I am treated so much differently than I was as a man. For one thing, men often open doors for me, which is a nice bonus, and makes me feel great. Interestingly, I have tried to break the gender rules by opening doors for guys, but they always look at me with a funny expression when I do it, as if to say, "What the hell do you think you're doing? That's my job!"

There is an underlying current of energy exchanged between the sexes that I didn't really realize until after transition. One day I was shopping at the local supermarket, and I was on the phone with Anvil. We were talking about all the kinds of food that he likes, and what he wanted to eat when he comes to visit. As I was picking out some avocados, I caught a glimpse of a big guy in shorts and a t-shirt with spiky black hair. He looked like a jock, like a guy who'd be on the offensive line of a football team. He was actually kind of cute, but he was too big and not my type. He was about twenty feet away, and I realized he was staring at me, and I mean staring at me, hardcore! I don't think he could have been more obvious about it. It was one of those, "you're hot, and so am I! I want you now!" stares, which I've come to recognize. I bagged my avocados and put them in my cart. I looked back at him, and he was walking sideways, still staring. I turned away and said to Anvil, "This guy is totally staring at me. It's freaking me out!" Anvil laughed. I moved my cart on down the aisle. The guy had moved away from me, but as I took one last glance at him, I saw that he was still staring at me, but that was the last time I saw him.

I am pretty sure he was staring at me not because he could tell I had transitioned but because he was attracted to me. It happens from time to time, which is a fantastic verification of who I am, and very uplifting. It's still something that takes a bit of getting used to, but I love it when it happens. It can also feel uncomfortable, as was the case on this particular day. When I was a guy, I never got looks like that from women. Women just don't do that. In fact, I didn't even know how women look at guys when they're attracted to them; I never noticed it. Interestingly, Cindy told me that she noticed girls looking at me all the time back when we were together, but I had been oblivious to it.

When I got home, I realized how funny this situation was: if this exact same encounter had happened back when I was in my twenties, when I looked like a man, it would have meant that the guy wanted to kick my ass! But now, it meant that the guy probably wanted to…dare I say, do something else with my ass. This is just one example of how men can treat women as objects, rather than as people. It feels weird to be looked at and desired as a sex object that way, although I must admit, coming from the right man, it can be extremely exciting! In my experiences being both sexes, this is one unspoken rule of gender engagement that has taken me some time to get used to, but I do enjoy it.

I have a theory, based on my experience of being involved

in so many male environments and my experience as a woman, that men have a "categorization system" for women. That is, when they see a woman for the first time, they put her in one of two categories: attractive and not attractive. If the woman falls in the first category, then the man admires her objectively and sexually, and he has a hard time focusing his attention on anything but his desire for her. If she falls into the second category then he generally seems to disregard her, or at the least acknowledge her for her intellectual or technical abilities. This may be a widely stereotyping theory, but as I ponder it during my day-to-day experiences with others, it seems to make sense.

As a man, when I would discuss cars, guitars, electronics, politics, or sports, for example, men would often give me the respect of listening to what I had to say and would at least act as though they believed I knew what I was talking about. If I were talking about dismantling a carburetor, they had a look on their face that told me they were listening, and that they respected my opinion.

As a woman, when I have talked to men about fixing cars, or building guitars, I find that their faces give away the fact that they just don't think I know what I'm talking about. Having experienced many interactions as both genders, I have noticed a definite difference in the way men relate to women, and vice versa.

Most men appear to not give women respect on an intellectual level overall. If they do, it is far less than they seem to give the men with whom they interact. Even if they're not sexually attracted to us, they still treat us as objects in so many ways, so much so that I think most of them fail to see the people we really are.

Sexism can be a very subtle form of emotional manipulation. I had never encountered it before transition, and since then I have encountered it a number of times at work. It is a tricky thing: most of the time it is so subtle that a person can't really do anything about it. If I were to say something to the man doing it, he would probably laugh at me and tell me I'm imagining things. But I've dealt with enough stuff like this to know what's what, and even if I can't do something official about it, I can at least deal with it on my own pretty well.

The changes I have experienced in my journey have been social, physical, and psychological. Now that I have had surgery, I've realized some of the interesting differences between male and female body parts. One of the main surgical results we seek is that we want our vagina to most closely resemble the placement of skin and genital parts of the natal female. After having surgery I have concluded that my doctor must do an excellent job of getting things where they should be, because everything feels so right. Of course, I don't personally have anything else to compare to, but after studying what he did and feeling, looking around, and exploring, I have to say that it all seems totally normal to me. I wouldn't change a thing about it.

There are some interesting differences between having a penis, scrotum, and testicles, and having a vagina. You can probably imagine what it is like to have the genitals of the opposite sex, but I'll bet there are some things you wouldn't think about. For example, both sexes have pubococcygeal (PC) muscles. These are the muscles around the opening of the pubic bone through which either the penis emerges from the body, or the vagina enters the body. You may have heard of Kegel exercises, which are used to strengthen these muscles for better sex.

The PC muscles in a male perform an extra function that they do not do in women, and that is to squeeze the flesh of the penis and urethra, thus stopping the flow of urine, or alternatively, helping to squirt out the last drops of pee. Females do not have this option because the urethra ends before it reaches the PC muscles. Although the muscles might be used to restrain urine or fluid in the vagina, the effect is not quite the same.

My skeletal size has not changed much, if any, but the way I carry myself has, which can make me appear at least one inch shorter than when I stand straight up. Back against a wall, standing straight up, I used to be about six-foot, one and one-half inches tall. When I cock my hip out to the side and arch my back slightly, I can drop down to just about six feet tall. Certain movements, like walking, are totally different than they used to be. Standing, walking, and a variety of other more subtle movements and mannerisms are things I have consciously changed and are now just unconscious parts of who I am. Though in many ways it seems more like they were always there and just needed to be unlocked. During my years working as a deejay in the topless clubs, I spent several hours a day studying the motions, movements, gestures, and behaviors of women. I would often practice hand movements and motions in my car on the way home from work, and I would practice other movements, such as walking and talking, at home.

Although my skeleton hasn't changed much, my body fat distribution sure has, and not all of it to my liking. If only the fat that likes to accumulate on my stomach and waist would just go straight to my boobs, well, what more can I say? It is quite astonishing how hormones affect the way our bodies look and function. They affect our minds tremendously as well. The first thing I noticed after starting HRT was a feeling of near-euphoria and calm. It seemed like the edginess of the world had been softened, and I just felt great. My theory is that this happened because the male and female brains, like gasoline and diesel engines, need the right fuel to run properly. When I started HRT, I finally felt as if I were on the right fuel.

One of the first physical changes I noticed after starting HRT was tenderness under my nipples, which was extremely exciting because it meant that my breasts were finally starting to grow. After wondering why they weren't growing back in my youth, and then finally feeling them start to grow almost twenty-nine years later, I was so excited! After that, I noticed that my skin softened a lot, and it seemed to have a glow to it, but it also dried out more easily. So lotions and Chap-Stick have become my close companions. I have also experienced minute changes in body hair: it thinned a lot on my torso, and some on my legs, but not much. Hormones have absolutely no effect on facial hair, which is somewhat disappointing, but definitely not a big deal considering the options that exist for that. The hair was easily removed with twenty-seven hours of electrolysis and another dozen or so laser treatments.

The change to my voice was, perhaps, one of the most challenging and personally nerve-racking parts of the entire transition process for me. Although now I have people tell me that my voice is one of my strongest assets, having such a voice hasn't come without a substantial amount of work. I started off with a very deep and powerful voice, which was great for belting out the lyrics to "Bitter End" and various heavy metal songs. When I was in my phase of trying to be the most macho guy possible, I had tried to ensure that my voice was as deep and as loud as it could be. When I first transitioned, the mother of one of Anvil's schoolmates said, "Of all the things about the old you I'm going to miss the most, it is your voice. It was so manly and sexy!" I just had to laugh.

The last thing I wanted was to be a girl with a guy's voice. So I practiced and practiced and practiced, all on my own. I practiced a lot in my car, because I could listen to and repeat the things that women said on the radio. That helped a lot. Television was a great way to practice, too. I found that recording a show on video tape was invaluable. I would watch mouths as I recited the words and tried to match pitch, tone, and inflection. I could rewind as much as I needed to, and it worked fantastically well. My second job in Austin was doing telemarketing work. Talk about freaking out! I was sure someone would "sir" me, but in the course of at least 20,000 phone conversations, guess how many times I got "sir'd"? Only once! And that one time, the female caller said, "Ooops! I'm sorry!" Funny how I went from being a macho deejay on a microphone saying things like "C'mon guys! Let's get a little love going on out there. Break those dollars free from your wallets and help out the ladies!" to the sweet and feminine, "Hello, this is Annah with UberTech; may I speak with John Doe please?" I tell you, life can be a trip! You just have to enjoy the ride.

All of these experiences have combined to create the overall picture of who I am, which is far more feminine than I used to be. Sitting, walking, running, leaning, driving—all are different now. It has taken me years of work to undo the effects of testosterone, time and social conditioning, but it has been worth it. To be beyond the transsexual condition and finally in my own skin is simply blissful.

The Ultimate Change

Many people who are uneducated about this subject have an assumption about genital reconstructive surgery. The best way to explain it may be to use the example of a question I was asked by one of my old band mates:

"So, you really want to have it cut off?" he asked.

It took me a moment to compose myself after the shock of hearing him say this, and to get my thoughts together for a proper response, for I knew quite well by this time that "cut off" was hardly what happens during GRS. Yes, there are some bad surgeons in the world who basically cut it off and leave a simple hole there. That is horrible, and I hope that trans women do not support doctors who do such butchery. Even worse, though, are the surgeons who have little or no experience in GRS and literally destroy a trans woman's chances of ever having a proper vagina.

There are doctors, however, who perform outstanding genital reconstruction using nearly every part of the penile and scrotal skin to create a fully sensitive and completely orgasmic vagina.

I spent years researching GRS on the Web and in print—reading the stories of girls who have been to various surgeons throughout the world. In my quest for the best doctor, with the limited perspective I had, I found a common consensus: a surgeon in Montreal, Dr. Pierre Brassard, was performing the most aesthetically pleasing and physically stimulating vaginoplasty in the world, and he was doing it using a one-step process.

One day, I had lunch with Donna, Julie, and three other post-op women. I was the only pre-op there, and I was still in the process of trying to choose a doctor, even though I had not yet determined how I would be able to afford the cost. I asked them all who they had gone to, and four of the five said that they had been to Dr. Brassard. I asked them what they thought of the experience, and they were unanimous: Brassard rocked their worlds. They were all incredibly happy with the results, and that was it for me. Decision made. All I had to do next was figure out how to pay for it.

The next year or so I worked hard and tried to save money,

though I was having a rough time of it because I wasn't able to get a solid, decent-paying job right away, and it was becoming apparent that I might never get a job at a company doing Web development or database work again. As the months passed and as I struggled along, I began to grow more and more depressed. The stuff between my legs was a constant reminder of what still needed to be fixed and how incomplete I felt. It also barred me from being social with men because I did not want that to be a factor. I figured they would probably be disgusted with the fact that I did not have a vagina, I know I felt that way. Most of all, I just wanted to be complete and comfortable with myself.

It had been quite some time since I had spoken to my parents. We had times when we drifted in and out of each other's' lives, for whatever reasons. It had been quite a long time since I had heard from them, but finally that all changed. One day, I was practicing with Boneglove at a place about twenty miles east of Austin. It was always a nice drive home after a grueling session out there. I was just passing the Austin Bergstrom International Airport, when my cell phone rang.

"Hello?" I said.

"Annah!" a female voice said with enthusiasm.

"Uh, hey!" I said, uncertain who it was.

"This is your Mom!" Mom said. I was shocked. It had been a long time. She proceeded to tell me that they had been talking about something for a few months and wanted to tell me that they had decided to pay for my GRS! I was incredibly excited and nearly drove right off the road! Life had been getting more distressing for me for the year or so prior to that day, because I was beginning to realize that there was not much likelihood of funding the costs for surgery on my own. This was such incredible news, not only because it meant that I was going to have the surgery, and that they would help me pay for it, but that both my parents were feeling okay with me and were supportive of what I had to do. An incredible sense of relief came over me. During the days following, I set my appointment with Doctor Brassard. It was to be September 23, 2004, which was about two years away.

They seemed like the longest two years ever, but my date for surgery came up fast. Between the time I set my appointment and the months before the date, I left Boneglove and became the guitar player in a band called Red Volution. At first I did not tell them about being trans. I figured it was really not necessary, at least not right away. Besides, it was nice just being myself and not having to rehash the past with them. Then there was the mild fear that they might not understand, but they had always been understanding guys, so I wasn't too worried about it.

During the year preceding my surgery, I was asked to do a *48 Hours* special, and while Donna was in town, we had dinner with the producer of the show. At that time, I was really unsure whether or not I wanted to do that particular show. It would have been a fifteen-minute segment, which is hardly enough time to get a point across, let alone discuss the deeper issues. There was also an air of sensationalism about it, not to mention the fact that they wanted me to change my surgery date to suit their schedule! I declined the offer. I still thought about the possibility of doing a show, though, and as fate would have it, the opportunity arose again.

A few months later, Donna told me that Discovery Health Channel was planning to do a piece that profiled a pre-op transsexual who was going in for surgery. They wanted to show the person before, during, and after the operation. The timing could not have been better, nor could the particular show and channel. I was very pleased to hear this and spoke with the producer of the show a few times over the phone. One day, I spoke with her from our band's rehearsal studio and told her I wasn't sure yet if I wanted to do the show, but it sounded like something I would be interested in. I was still unsure about going public about being trans, and I spent a lot of time pondering the idea.

One of the main reasons I decided to do the show was because I want so much to help others dealing with the transsexual condition, and the only way to do that successfully was to be visible. I knew that the show would bring excellent visibility, so that was a plus.

Another reason I decided to do it was because, since I was determined to be a successful musician, I figured that if I did eventually become successful, there was a great likelihood that I wouldn't be able to remain stealth. A journalist or someone would break the news as though they had gotten some dirt on me. I didn't want that. I wanted to be in control of how the world found out, or at least to be able to say that I had never hidden my past.

The show's producer told me on the phone that, if the band and I wanted them to, they would come by and shoot some footage of us jamming and put that in the show. That sounded like a pretty sweet deal! With all these positives, I couldn't foresee any negatives, other than the possibility of someone I worked with seeing it and freaking out, so I decided to do it. The only thing I needed to do was let the band know.

We were a couple of weeks into the process of recording our first album, *Dark Matter*, when the time came. As often is the case, it was not so much the time of my choosing as much as it was just the right time. I had previously told the guys that I was taking a vacation to Montreal for a few weeks at the end of September, and they were fine with that. But one day during a recording session, our singer asked me if I could play a gig on October 8. I said, "I don't think I'll be ready to do that."

"Why?" he asked. "Are you going to see old friends or family and come back all depressed or something?"

"No," I said, contemplating. Then I realized it was time.

"I'll be recovering from surgery," I told him.

"Surgery?" he said, his eyes widening. "For what? Do you have cancer? Are you okay?"

I laughed. "No, no cancer," I said, "And yes, I'm okay. In fact, I'm going there for some very positive surgery." He inquired further.

"I'm having genital reconstructive surgery," I said. I told him, as well as our bass player, who had just come into the room. They were both surprised. It made me feel great to know that they really had no idea I was trans. Our drummer came in a few minutes later, and I told him the news, too. He said, "So...uh, what are you coming back with?" I laughed and thanked him, saying that was the best compliment I'd had in ages! We discussed the transsexual condition and all that it entailed. Then I told them there was a possibility I would do the Discovery Health Channel show, "seXchange: Him to Her," and that if I did, there was an excellent chance that the crew would come out to shoot footage of the band. They got extremely excited about that idea, and said, "Hell, yeah! We'll do that!" They also told me that, no matter what, they supported me completely. I am so glad things worked out as well as they did with them.

Several weeks later, the television crew from Australia came to interview me and shoot footage of me throughout Austin. It was about a twelve-hour session of wandering around town, doing interviews at Town Lake and in Music Makers, one of the local music stores. The guys in the store were so cute; they asked what the hubbub was all about, and I told them. They were amazed and thought it was very cool. It was a tiring, but exciting and fun day. The interview was the last thing they shot, and I was wiped out by then. I slept so well that night. It was a great day.

The crew was going to be in Montreal the week of my surgery and planned to shoot footage of me before, during, and after surgery. I was very excited about that. They asked if I had anyone else, family or friends, coming to be with me during the surgery, and I said I did not. They had previously asked if Cindy would be interested in doing an interview, but she wasn't sure. They asked if I thought she might like to come up to Montreal to be with me and to be interviewed. I said I didn't know, but I'd ask. They offered to pay for her flight and lodging, so she said she would be happy to do it.

The time in Montreal was incredible, and I will forever cherish the brief bit of time I spent there. The residence where I stayed is no longer in operation, which is very sad; it was a beautiful place to stay. But, as of this writing, Dr. Brassard still performs surgeries in Montreal, and there is another residence now that is closer to the hospital.

We arrived on Tuesday, and Cindy's flight arrived only about an hour after mine. I sat in the airport with my bag and felt like a foreigner for the first time in my life. Everyone was speaking French. It was very strange, yet very exciting. There was a strange humility I felt during that hour, and it was very interesting watching and listening to people, trying to figure out what they were talking about. I expect someone must have said, "Ha ha! Look at her; she has no idea what we are saying!"

Cindy arrived and looked stunning, as always. It was great to see her—it had been quite some time since we had seen each other last. We hugged and made our way out to the curb; we called the limo driver, and he picked us up. Oddly, he had a woman passenger in the front seat with him. As we were leaving the airport, she asked the driver if he were

going to such-and such a place. He said no, that he was going somewhere else. As it turned out, she had gotten in the wrong limo! We had to turn back around and take her back to the airport. Cindy and I laughed in the back seat. It was an odd way to get back together for the first time in ages, but it was exciting and fun.

When we arrived at the residence, we met a few of the other girls; some were pre-op, some were post-op. We spent some time hanging out, talking and watching the *Rocky Horror Picture Show* on DVD and laughing a lot. The next day was spent getting things ready and going to the hospital, where I spent the night before surgery. Cindy stayed in a nearby hotel.

While in Montreal I met seventeen other transsexual women during my thirteen days there. All of us were in consensus that one of the main reasons we were there, aside from Dr. Brassard's excellent reputation, was that he does a one step process. Many GRS surgeons perform a two-step process, which requires a patient to go into surgery for the initial vaginoplasty, and then return approximately three months later for more work, which is usually the labiaplasty. This second procedure is meant to give a more natural and aesthetically appearing vagina. If you ask me, going in for surgery on my genitals once is enough. Besides, when you can go to a doctor like Brassard and have a beautiful, fully functional vagina created in one session, there is just no other choice. In addition, the pre- and postoperative care in Montreal was second to none.

The next morning, the day of surgery, was brief for me. They woke me up, and told me to get changed and to get on a nearby gurney. Then they rolled me out of the hospital room and down the hall to the elevator; we went up a few floors to the surgery level. I was temporarily stationed in a very dim room. I was very excited, but very relaxed. A moment passed; then they put a cap on my head and rolled me into the surgery room. All I remember was looking up at the huge light fixture above me; it was seven huge lights in one. The anesthesiologist told me I'd feel a slight sting in my arm. "Okay," I said, gazing up at the lights. "That sure is one ominous light…"

While I was in surgery, Cindy did her interview for the Discovery Health show. The next thing I knew, I was waking up in my hospital bed, and Cindy was stroking my forehead and hair.

"It's all over, Annah," she said. "They're all done. You can be at peace now." Of all the people in the world to be there, she was the one I wanted. I wished that Anvil could have been there, too, though. I don't know that I can thank her enough for being there. It meant so much to me, so incredibly much.

I spent a few days in recovery at the hospital. There was a massive ice pack on my crotch for a few days. It needed constant changing, but that and all of the other things I had to do were nothing compared to how incredibly happy I felt. Cindy had to head home the day after surgery, but I got to spend lots of wonderful time with my roommate and the other two girls who had had surgery the same day. We had become a brand-new family, like sisters, brought together from different parts of the world to that one place and time, to finally right the wrongs that we lived with for so long. After a few days at the hospital, we all headed back to the residence.

The week and a half I spent at the residence following surgery was perhaps the most rewarding aspect of the entire experience. We spent a lot of time sitting on our little "donuts" that kept our sore spots off the hard surfaces. We ate a lot of great meals prepared by the staff, and we took many baths, to keep our new parts clean. At first you have what can only be likened to the stitches in a football, which hold in the "turkey stuffing" that keeps the walls of the vagina in place while you heal. After a few days, Dr. Menard, who is Dr. Brassard's business partner, came in with a nurse and removed those stitches. Getting them out was no fun, but it was a welcome relief. After a few days, those huge stitches really began to pull on my skin and hurt.

Leaving the residence and going home was a mixture of happiness and sadness. I was so excited to be beyond the surgery, and I had made so many new friends, which I would miss very much. Some of us exchanged numbers and email addresses and headed back, one by one, each in our own direction. Flying home was okay. I was sore, but it wasn't too painful. I got home and enjoyed another week off before returning to work. Post-op care is intense. You have to dilate a lot, to make sure the vagina doesn't collapse on itself and to ensure it maintains its depth and width. This needs to be done five times a day in the beginning, and then it tapers off over time.

When I was two weeks post-op, I still had some minor swelling of the labia minora and some mild soreness around my pubic area, but the results were incredible! The changes I went through during those two weeks—physical, mental, and emotional changes—were profoundly positive. Since the day of my surgery, I have been incredibly happy, and finally a feeling of peace came over me that I had never experienced before. As the days and weeks passed by, as the swelling subsided, and as the nerve endings reconnected, the new arrangement of my genital parts has become a source of seemingly unending new and wonderful sensations.

The most noticeable sensation was when nerves reconnected from tissue to tissue. The feeling was kind of like what would happen if you held a 9-volt battery on your tongue, only this was between my legs! Not only are these sensations intense and random, but they can happen anywhere.

One day, about three weeks post-op, I was at a popular warehouse store, cruising down the aisles and looking for chocolate, when all of a sudden I had wave after wave of nerve jolts hit me. I had to stop and hold on to my cart. I found myself bent over the cart, grasping it with both arms while my body twitched and contorted with each wave that ran through me. Not only did the waves affect my genitals, but they also affected my entire body, causing full-body contortions along with occasional vocal squeaks and moans. It was a good thing there were not many people in the store that day, but when I figured I could start walking again, I looked up to see a couple down the isle looking at me with interest. My actions must have thrown them for a loop. I was so moved that I completely forgot to get the chocolate.

One of the main tasks a new post-op girl has to do each day is dilate. This is the insertion of hard plastic dilators into the vagina. The dilators resemble vibrators, but without the vibrations. They come in various sizes, the smallest of which are about a half inch in diameter, and the largest are about an inch and a quarter to an inch and a half in diameter. I started with the smallest one first and slowly worked my way up to the ones with larger diameters. It may seem small, but at first that half-inch diameter feels like the size of a damn cannon! During the first several weeks after surgery, dilating is not the most fun thing in the world, but once sensation returns, and you don't have to dilate every day, then the process becomes far less of a chore and far more fun. Then, of course, one finds pleasure in "toys" of all shapes and sizes, many of which can be made from household items. I am sure many women have tried different kinds of things, but it is amazing to think about this—the next time you're in the grocery store, especially in the wine and oriental sauces isles, take a look at those "special" bottle shapes! You'll be quite intrigued, and perhaps excited, by many of the unique styles and shapes they come in!

The process of dilation helps the walls of the new vagina attach to the inner body and keeps the vagina from closing in on itself. It also keeps the opening wider and deeper, which is absolutely necessary for anyone considering having intercourse later on. After about a year post-op, I only had to dilate once every week or two.

In my quest to understand my new sexuality, I looked at a popular women's Web site about dating, men, sex, and relationships. The site mentioned that for women, having an emotional link to the man they are with is profoundly important during sex. Some say that it is even more important than the sex itself, and, after my experience, I believe this to be true. Sex as a woman is absolutely awesome and exceeds all my expectations. I must say, I can thoroughly understand the need for foreplay now. Sex for a woman is highly emotional, mental, and, dare I say, spiritual. Or perhaps that is my perspective of it now, since I have experienced both sides. I have finally experienced that which I have desired all my life, and it simply rocks!

Since completing transition and surgery, my goal for sexual experience has shifted dramatically. In fact, my whole attitude about sex has changed. I don't want to be with just any man I find attractive; I want to be with one to whom I have a deep emotional attachment, too. I find that passion and emotion are just as important as the physical act of sex. While sex is exciting and feels great, there is something lacking if there is no emotional bond as well. So I can forgo having sex just to have sex. Now I will wait until I meet the right guy. If that never happens, well, so be it. I still have my toys!

Sex for me now has been very interesting to experience, because there was a time when I did just enjoy sex for its own sake. I believe that estrogen has played a critical role in these changes. Not only does estrogen affect a woman's body physically, it affects a woman's mind tremendously in many different ways. It makes women more emotional, for one thing. For men and trans men, testosterone has an incredible effect on libido. Surely, no longer having testosterone in my body has affected my libido as well as my perspective on sex and relationships. Rather than having sex just for the sake of sex (or for the orgasm) it is more about the intimacy between myself and my partner. It is a way of feeling closer on an emotional level, as well as a way to be as close as physically possible, both of which I find very sexually arousing.

The Discovery Health Channel show aired several months after my surgery. It was a very exciting time. Many of my friends and family recorded it, and since it aired, I have received countless e-mails from people all over the world thanking me for having the courage to do the show, for being visible, and for helping others. I had no idea just how far-reaching that show would be, and I am constantly amazed, and very grateful, for the positive response I have received because of it. I have not once regretted doing it.

That show has aired at least several times since the first showing, and it seems like each time it airs someone new says to me, "Hey, I saw you on Discovery Channel. That was amazing!" And it makes me feel really good. To think, back when I was young I thought people would ridicule me for who I am, and now I find them thanking me and telling me how amazed they are with my courage!

The Power of Intention

During the past several years, a distinct underlying force has made itself apparent to me more and more as I've delved deeper into the psychology of transsexualism and gender. The force I've noticed is the incredible power of *intention*.

There is an amazing energy that comes from intention, like an invisible laser beam or a magnifying glass focusing a pinpoint of sunlight on a piece of paper. The origin of intention is in our minds, our hearts, and our spirits, and the target can be anything—person, place, thing, or even ourselves and our goals. Intention can have a positive or negative charge, like any energy, and can be used for good or bad. We may not often think of intention as being such a strong force in our lives, but it is a distinct aspect of who we are and what we do.

In order to affect change in our lives, we must have intentions. We intend to go to the store to pick up some food. We intend to get gasoline on the way to work. We intend to throw a party for our friend's birthday. We intend to start that project we have been putting off.

Intention, like any force, has differing levels of power. The energy of some intentions is very weak, and those intentions are not in the forefront of our thoughts, or at the top of our list of things to do. They get moved to the backburner, and other energies take the driver's seat. Some intentions have incredible power, such as our drive to achieve our dreams and goals, or to become outstanding at the things we are passionate about and the things we love to do. Passion is surely the rocket fuel for our intentions.

One of the biggest problems I think we often run into is a lack of intention. I believe this is tied very intimately with complacency, for if we were not complacent, then our intentions would take more of a front seat in our lives and we would empower them even more and make more things happen in our lives.

Intention, to me, has been strongest in a few aspects of my life. For example, ever since I started playing guitar, I intended to be the best in the world; I wanted to be well known, and highly regarded and respected as a guitar player. I wanted people to look up to me for my skills and talents in that regard. Why? Glory? Fame? Money? Definitely not money, interestingly enough. The most important thing to me was to be loved for what I love to do; material rewards haven't been a focus in any of the things I do.

As my life has changed, and as I have accepted who I am and done the things necessary to become myself, I have observed my own changing intentions. The more I have revealed myself to the world, beginning with being visible on the Internet, then participating in the Discovery Health Channel show *"seXchange: Him to Her"*, and now writing my book, I can look at myself and see that my general intentions in life have evolved from just wanting to be myself and play my guitar to being myself, playing my guitar, and helping others. The main focus of my intent to help others encompasses a desire not only to help other trans people, but to help the world at large understand us better, and realize that we are not freaks or perverts, that we are just regular people.

One of the things I find interesting is how intention is tied to change. Change, as we all know, is really the only constant in our lives, yet we have this funny desire to try to keep it at bay. We don't like change, for the most part, especially when we are forced to change. For example, when a person changes his or her sex, that person is forcing the other people in their lives to change in many significant ways. Parents of transsexuals may not want that kind of change in their lives, but if they don't want to lose their child forever, then they must accept things as they are, and acceptance is a pivot point of change. As much as we don't want to, sometimes we have to change how we relate to ourselves, to each other, and to the world. One person's intention is another person's uninvited change.

For most of my life I knew that something about myself needed to be changed, although I didn't know what that was for a long time. Once I realized what it was, I knew what the change was that I needed to make, but I couldn't find enough energy to power the intention to change. There were forces in me that were keeping me from changing: guilt, shame, and fear. Those emotions are like walls that keep us from doing what we know we need to do. They block the energies that would otherwise fuel our intentions to change. Eventually, we reach a point where something happens, something "clicks," or we experience a trauma of some kind that often subconsciously provides us with the power to break down those mental barriers and finally take action.

What I have found to be the key to my success in overcoming the conundrum of gender dysphoria is my unquenchable desire to be happy and at peace with myself, no matter what I have to do in order to obtain and maintain this state of inner peace. I believe I only get one life to live and I'll be damned if I'm going to waste it by being unhappy for the sake of others! Of course, this doesn't mean that I would hurt or take advantage of other people to get what I want. What I mean is that I won't let fear, shame, embarrassment, or any of those walls block my quest for fulfillment in life. I will not let myself keep myself down. I finally know what I want: I want to be me, and I want to be successful at helping others be themselves, too. I want to be successful at helping them, their friends, their families, and anyone else who is curious, to understand what we go through. I want to do this simply because I want to help others have a better life, be happy, and find peace.

It's funny how sometimes we have to overcome so much before we can get on with our lives and the things we want to achieve.

Despite the sexual revolution, the advent of feminism, greater numbers of men and women in nontraditional roles and jobs, the basic expectations have not changed: male still equals masculine and powerful; female equals feminine and submissive. The National Organization of Women online contains a wide array of information about how the roles of men and women have and have not changed throughout the years. As far as our overall society has been concerned, however, this separation of gender roles is still a core aspect of our social expectations. You either live in one box or the other, like it or not, and if you're different and you don't fit in, then you'd better just shut up about it and act like everybody else. These boxes have been defined, in large part, by nature, simply because there are two distinct sexes. However, I suspect that it is because of that very nature that we make the incorrect assumption that there are no variations of the two.

Historically, the wedge between the sexes has been driven deeper by society and its seemingly ever-increasing need to define the two sexes. Not only has general society had a major role in this division, but so too have many facets of religion, which has not only driven wedges between the sexes, but between what is considered right and wrong. For many religions and right-wing political organizations, homosexuality, transsexuality, bisexuality, and any variation thereof, are proclaimed "sinful" and "amoral". In fact, just recently the President of the United States, George W. Bush, defined marriage as "a union between a man and a woman" and in June of 2006 stated in his weekly radio address, "Marriage is the most enduring and important human institution, honored and encouraged in all cultures and by every religious faith," This statement does nothing but alienate those people who do not fall within the confines of the religious boundaries that he referred to. Additionally, they do nothing more than inflict the whip of shame, guilt, and fear upon people who should not be punished for who they are, but rather, embraced and supported because they live in a world that berates them for being who they are. For *who they are*. If marriage truly is the "most enduring and important human institution" then should not *all* human beings have a right to it?

I know that many people who read the Bible and practice their religious beliefs do not believe that people like us are wrong or sinful, but there is a major movement of the "religious right" that most surely is trying very hard to squelch anyone and everyone who does not fit into the tiny boxes where they believe everyone should fit. It angers me greatly to be accused of being sinful, evil, or "choosing to be this way," especially when these charges are made by people who do not even know me. It makes me realize just how limited their perspective is, and how the blinders their religion has placed on them affects their outlook on life and other human beings. So many do not see or accept human diversity, and that is the saddest loss of all, for we are each unique and special, and each of us has value to offer. I do not hold their accusations against them, nor do I judge them because of what they say and do. I do not understand their beliefs, but I would not attack their very right to exist because of *who they are*. I simply wish they could have a live-and-let-live attitude toward others, rather than feeling they have a right to define human nature. To me, that, and their judgment of others, seems to be opposed to what they say they believe in. My purpose is not to attack religion; but this is what is happening in the world around me, and I feel that it is important that it be mentioned and discussed. I am sure there are people much better equipped to discuss this issue than I am. Even with that, I still have the right to express how I see things from my perspective because it affects me directly: I am one of the people they judge to be sinful and amoral, yet I know the real truth, that I am neither. I simply *am.*

For many of us, in order to fit in with the world around us, we push down, repress, and hide what we are feeling and who we are. People who are anti-anything that doesn't fit the mold try to label people who don't fit into neat boxes as social deviants, freaks, or outcasts. I suppose it is their right to believe such absurdities as that, and sometimes I ask myself why I would even want to live in a world where there are so many people who think that way. Those people appear so close minded and lacking of compassion, perhaps they are repressing more than they would care to admit. I'm not out to start a fight; rather, I want to just open eyes and minds, in an effort to bring fairness and balance to all. I believe that it is important to point out this common attitude, for if no one points it out, it runs rampant and only gets worse. We have an obligation, to ourselves and to humanity as a whole, to address hatred, fear and discrimination, especially when it is used to push a political agenda.

Because of such intense external influences telling us that who we are is wrong, it sometimes seems easier to repress who we are than to face the truth and go with our natural flow. We don't want to let our parents, family, or friends down by admitting we're not what they think we are. So rather than risk emotional (and sometimes physical) pain, we repress our thoughts, our feelings, and our selves, never knowing what impact that repression will have on us. At times we become so good at repressing that we believe our problems are gone. But they always come back, and they usually come back even stronger than before. It is a vicious cycle, a broken melody from an instrument that is out of tune, in disharmony with itself and thus in disharmony with the symphony of life. Yet somehow we can't seem to find the proper way to tune our instruments. We lose the meaning of happiness as it becomes hidden under the waves of repression; we lose who we are supposed to be, but are not.

People can only hide themselves from themselves for so long before the critical threshold is reached. The key to dealing with any kind of repression is to acknowledge the issues, admit them, face them, and *deal with them.* Only then can we fix the problems plaguing us and find the true meaning of happiness in our lives.

Never Rule Out Your Dreams

I can hardly believe that I am now living two of my life-long dreams: I'm finally the woman I needed to be, and I have finally had sex the way I have always wanted it. Let's make that three dreams, because if you're reading this, it means that another life-long dream of mine has come true, and that is to be a published author. And wait! There's one more, I'm now in the world's coolest metal band!

Many people in my life now know about my history. None of the people in Austin knew me before transition, but most knew me before they knew I dealt with the transsexual condition. More people I meet now seem to know, but they are usually friends of those who already know, I guess. But there are a lot of people I meet who have no idea who I am or anything about my past, and I must say that I like that a lot. It feels like a more even playing field, socially speaking, because all I ever wanted was to just be me, a woman.

It's interesting how some of the guys I've known for a couple of years treat me differently now that they know, and overall they're really cool about it. Except for being sort of standoffish when they saw me after they found out, they treat me the way I have seen them treat other women, which I am learning has its ups and downs. Being a girl in the music industry is very different from being a guy in it. Now that I'm getting more accustomed to being myself, I can pay more attention to how the world around me treats me. It's very interesting, to say the least. It is not something one really thinks about when pondering changing sex, and it is not something most people think much about at all, I would bet.

Some of the best examples of this are when I go into music stores to look at guitars or amps, or to buy new strings or picks. At first, salesmen assume that I am either just wandering around while my boyfriend shops for a guitar, or that I might be buying one for someone else. I was once asked if I was buying my boyfriend a guitar for Christmas! I enjoy playing along with their game and sometimes I play dumb, asking if I can plug one in and check it out. They try to direct me toward some cheap amp or guitar. I tell them, "No, I'd like to plug *that* one into *that* amp and see what it sounds like." as I point to a USA Jackson Rhoads and a Marshall stack. They usually raise an eyebrow and oblige, apparently eager to see what happens. I then commence to crank up and blow their minds with my twenty-plus years of heavy metal guitar playing experience! They are usually quite shocked, which gives me great pleasure. When I worked at Guitar Center I could usually draw a pretty good crowd of onlookers. I think that is the main reason they decided to let me go, even though they said it was because my gross profit wasn't high enough. Or, perhaps it was a combination of both.

Even though I enjoy standing out from the crowd and sometimes being the center of attention, one of the things that I have never wanted to be was a complete outcast. I don't mind being weird or different necessarily; in fact, all my life people have told me I was weird, and I relish my weirdness because it means I am unique. Nonetheless, I didn't want to be looked at as some kind of freak or anomaly. There is not much social freak ground left for people, but those of us who have changed our sex are apt to be considered freaks if we don't blend in or pass well. Things are getting better for us, though, more so as time passes. I think that every human being has the same feelings overall—we all want to fit in, one way or another.

I had always hoped to be able to integrate as a normal woman in society. It's very hard sometimes when you're a young person looking at the world through the eyes of the wrong gender. You have to go with it at first. You try to keep up appearances. You dress the part, walk the walk, and talk the talk. It becomes routine and easy. You get complacent with it, and you tell yourself it's a phase, that everyone feels this way. You decide for sure that every boy you know must feel the same way you do, it's just that no one ever talks about it. Then one day you realize that not everyone else feels this way, and in fact that maybe no one else feels this way. You get lonely. You get scared. You begin to withdraw, or you escape by pouring your soul into something creative—art, music—and as you express yourself through your art form, a picture of who you are slowly becomes clearer and clearer to you. You are creating yourself in your art, and one day you realize that who you are isn't really who you are, and the gears in your head begin to turn, and you get all crazy wondering what the hell is wrong with you. After hours, months, years of research and lots of self-evaluation, you find solace in the fact that you really aren't the only one after all. In fact, there are thousands, even tens of thousands, of people just like you.

Suddenly, you don't feel so much like a freak. Suddenly, you don't feel so alone in the world. Suddenly, you meet people who can relate to you and share your frustration and confusion. Incredibly, you see a light at the end of the tunnel— that tunnel that you have been trapped in for so many years. And one day you find yourself, as you step out into the sunshine.

It wasn't until recently that the true meaning of the phrase, "Can't see the forest for the trees," finally made sense to me. I realized that I was so focused on the little things—the little hairs I had to pluck, the size of my boobs, surgery, clothes, makeup, hair— as I tried to get to my goal, as I tried to get rid of the maleness that surrounded me. But as I stood and looked at my naked self in the mirror, I saw not a single trace of it, and I was in awe. I turned around and still saw no signs, and then I believed what people had been telling me for so long: I don't look transsexual; I look female. It was always hard for me to believe that, and now maybe I have realized that it was because I doubted myself, or because I wasn't sure yet, or still had lingering doubts about how I passed, but I think it came down to acceptance. I finally accepted the fact that I am now, indeed, a woman.

What I have hope for the most in the future is that I can provide a strong example of how we really are, and how little there is about us for people to be afraid of. Additionally, people need to understand that people like me are not the anomaly they thought we were. We are quite common, actually, and we should be understood and accepted, for we, too, are a natural part of this human race.

My future is as wide open as the great countryside. I have a few goals in life, the primary one being to have a successful career playing heavy metal guitar, as well as to help those like me who are struggling to overcome the often oppressive feelings that come with such a unique gift. I also want to provide for my son and my family as best I can; how I will do that, exactly, I do not know, but I'm sure I'll find a way. Or perhaps…a way will find me. I have my music, art, and writing, and I will never stop creating. Once this book is published, my focus will be to try to get it into as many hands as I can, and to try to help people understand that those of us who have to deal with the transsexual condition are nothing to be afraid of; we are just regular people trying to cope with our lives the best we can, just like everyone else.

In addition to the world recognizing us as people, too, I feel obligated to emphasize how important it is that we be true to who we are inside, the real self, the person who is in our mind, and the image of our dreams. We need to provide positive examples for the world to see, to prove that we are as deserving of respect and compassion as anyone else. It seems like we get so wrapped up in trying to live up to the expectations of those around us that we lose sight of who we really are, or who we want to be. When you were little, they asked you, "What do you want to be when you grow up?" Is what you answered what you are now? Or did you follow a different path and become someone else entirely? Satisfaction, happiness, love, and compassion—those are the things we need to be and to share with one another, not phony expectations and ideals based on outdated thinking styles. We need to accept each other for who we are, but more importantly we need to accept ourselves for who we are, for if we cannot be true to ourselves, who can we possibly be true to?

One of the hardest things to do is to put yourself on the line, to place who you are out there for the entire world to see, to face judgment and scrutiny about who you are. It takes a lot of inner strength and self-confidence to pull that off. Five years ago, I would never have been able to do it, but now, even though most of the people who know me know about me, it doesn't matter. I love myself, for the first time in my life, and I am proud of where I am and who I am, and that alone gives me the strength to stand up to anything at all. And if I can do that, anyone can do it! At the very least, we owe it to ourselves and to our loved ones to just simply be ourselves.

Without Me

There you are again, I've seen you before
Oh so many times
Standing there staring blankly at me
Who are you, why do you keep coming here
Invading my mind?
I don't know if you are me or who or which is what I see
Tell you you're fine and doin' good now
Workin' it out
Me I'm you and me you're there in my face
Spin around and hope to see myself again
Scream and shout
Spread myself thin and red all over the place
We end up on the evening news
Where in Hell did I leave my screws?
Now we're in a jam
We've been wrapped up like a Christmas ham
Lock me in the plush motel room
Though I can't see you, I can hear you
You were always with me, my friend one
Even there when I was alone
Scatter my past like confetti in the wind
As you drill into my soul
Take away from me my only friend
They leave me here by myself so alone now I'm feeling so
cold
I have nothing left of you but this scar on my head
This hole in my soul—Where are you?
This hole in my head—Why are you gone?
Why?
Where?
Who
Am I Without me?

The more time that passes since I transitioned, and especially since surgery, the more clarity and purity I feel in my life. Gone are the feelings of incongruence, confusion, and inner frustration. Gone are the deep and high roller-coaster rides of emotion. I don't walk through my days wondering who I am or what my purpose in life is, because now I have finally achieved my ultimate goal—to find and be myself. I guess most people don't have to worry about that so much; they get to just be themselves. But, I'm happy with who I am, where I've been, and what I've done with my life. I could die tomorrow, and I'd be fine with it. My life has meaning and purpose because now, for the first time in almost forty years, I am simply comfortable being me, and I love being me—finally!

As I write more and more, in my book and in my blog online, and as my interests evolve with my new perspective on life, I am seeing a path opening up before me. It is wide and bright, with the light of hope for an exciting future, rich with experience and pleasure that can only be enjoyed with a clear head and happy heart. It feels great to finally reach that point. And as I sit here and write this, as the world outside my little apartment's window rushes by, I wonder how many of those people out there have had to fight so long, so hard, and come so close to failure, just to be themselves. I am sure that there are many who feel this way. Perhaps people don't talk about it that much. For me, it happens to be right there on my sleeve, for the entire world to see.

To say there is a grand sense of relief and comfort within me now is actually an understatement. I feel great, better than ever, as if there is nothing I can't overcome. I feel empowered, as a woman, and as a human being. I feel stronger than ever and beautiful for the first time in my life. It has been a long, tough road to get where I am today, and it will not be an easy road from here to my next milestone, but after facing myself and conquering that which almost took me down, I fear nothing and no one. All I have to say to the world now is, "Bring it on, baby!"

Final Thoughts—The Last Piece of the Puzzle

All my life, until after transition and surgery, I felt like a rather jumbled pile of puzzle pieces, all mixed up, with no one to put them together. When I first started learning about gender and transsexual issues, and it became clear to me what was going on, I began to feel as if I could finally see the pictures on each piece, but they were still a mess. As I picked each one up and studied it, I could see a small piece of what it meant, and here and there, I was able to put a few of the pieces together. When I got help—counseling and support from others—I finally started to get the border of the puzzle that was me together, and an image of my true self began to grow clearer. The puzzle began to form an image, an image of myself, of who I was to become. Now, that puzzle is mostly complete; there are still a small number of pieces off to the side, waiting to be placed. I don't think the last piece will go in until my very last day, but as long as I can see most of the big picture of myself, I can't ask for anything more.

Being transsexual in this world is, in my opinion, one of the most challenging personal issues one can face. We are up against all kinds of stigmas that are rooted in misconceptions—assumptions that we are perverted, or that we want to change ourselves for sexual pleasure. There are misconceptions that we are somehow freaks, or that we are not real women. We are real women; our journey just got delayed and took a different course, and we have a few physical obstacles to overcome. There are misconceptions about gender and sexuality in general, such as the belief that everyone is born perfectly male or female. This is not the case! There are hundreds of thousands of people born transsexual or inter-sexed. Awareness of our plight needs to be raised, and it is, slowly but surely. Still, we have a long way to go and we need all the help we can get, especially from people outside the trans community.

Most people can hide their problems from the world as they walk about their daily routines, but we cannot. We wear our problem on our sleeves, on our faces, on our entire visible beings. With therapy, training, hormones, and surgery, we can come very close to never having to worry about others seeing the issues that have troubled us all our lives, but not all of us have the resources to make our dreams of finding ourselves a reality. My heart sinks and my chest hurts when I think of all the transsexual women I have met in the past few years who cannot afford to pay for facial feminization surgery, GRS, electrolysis, laser hair removal, or even for hormones. And our messed-up health care system isn't giving us a second thought.

It would be ideal if we had more options. surgeries need to be considered, by the health-care industry, not as a cosmetic or vanity surgery, but as a medically necessary surgery and part of a regimen for relief from the transsexual condition. We need health insurance companies to recognize this as well, and to make a commitment to helping us and treating us as they would treat any other person with legitimate health-care needs. We need health-care equality.

We are on our way, though, and I am proud of the progress we have made. I am eternally grateful to the many transsexual women and men who have laid bricks in the path that I have walked. And I am proud of myself, for I have laid some bricks in that path for the ones who will follow in my footsteps.

We all know how tough life can be sometimes. In addition to just surviving, achieving our dreams and goals is among the greatest challenges we face. Not only is the world full of uncertainties and dangers that may or may not directly affect us, but living our lives can pose incredible challenges. Often, during our daily struggles, it seems like our dreams are always just beyond our reach, and depending on how driven we are to reach them, we either keep climbing the mountains toward them, or we give up and settle into the complacency of mediocrity. That is not to say that mediocrity and complacency are all that bad; they just don't seem to push the envelope of human advancement all that much.

Besides the usual challenges that abound, we each face unique personal obstacles: physical health problems, mental problems, issues related to addiction, or any wide variety of other challenges. Some are easier to overcome than others, and some are simply habits that need to be changed. Sometimes there are issues that involve the very core of who are and what we are. These are issues that, if we choose to address them, may very well direct us on a path of complete and utter change, a reorganization of everything we are and all that we think we know— and all under the curious and often judgmental eyes of the world in which we live.

Our incredible universe is filled with rhythms and harmonies that extend throughout every nook and cranny of space and time as we know it. We base the very structure of our lives on frequencies of vibration: tones, melodies, harmonies, and rhythms, which coalesce together in a symphony of life that echoes through the vastness of our cosmos. In every possible way, music and rhythm play an incredibly important role in our lives. The substances that make up our flesh vibrate on all levels, from subatomic to infinitely huge. Our hearts beat in time with our emotions. Even our thoughts and actions have rhythms to them, which we may not even notice because we are so accustomed to them. As we grow older and gain experience in life, it takes time to find our own personal rhythms and to grow into them. Most of us flow into those rhythms naturally because there is a congruence between who and what we are; for some of us, however, the "who and what" may not match up properly, and we face the incredible challenge of having to figure out exactly who we really are underneath it all, who we need to be, and what we have to do to fix our conundrum.

When we find ourselves in incongruent circumstances, we find it hard, if not impossible, to be in tune with our own being. We struggle day and night, week by week and month by month, from the very first years of our lives, in an attempt to simply *be*: to be happy, to be as one within ourselves, to *start* our lives, to be able to move forward, to be able to *live*.

Personal discordance often rings through us so thoroughly that it alters our behavior and numbs our ability to understand, relate to, or be ourselves. In so doing, it discolors our view of the world around us: our trust, faith, and hope in life become diffused by a haze of confusion and self-doubt, which begins to swallow up our self-worth. How can we be in touch with anything, with *anyone*, in this world if we are not in touch with ourselves? It is my firm belief that we simply cannot.

We try and try again to find peace, to fit in with the world as it says we should. We go with the flow that our bodies define, but our minds, subconsciously or consciously, argue with what our bodies so blatantly state. As the years pass and the harmony within us becomes ever more askew and atonal, we become even more lost in the jumbled rhythms and melodies that block us from ourselves.

Being out of tune within our own being makes it so that we can hardly be in tune with anyone or anything else in the world. Our confusion evolves into frustration, anger, and depression, and oftentimes we go spiraling downward into a darkness that too often consumes us.

There is more to life than living in a waking dream. There is more to life than playing the role of a character with which you cannot identify. There is harmony. There is music. There is happiness. There is life to be *lived*—not just trudged through day by day, waiting, hoping, dreaming for something or someone to come along and make everything better. The reins of our lives are not meant to be taken by another; they are dangling right in front of us, and they are waiting for us to firm our resolve, grab them hard, and ride free!

Sometimes we need to wake up—open our eyes and look within at what makes us in or out of tune with ourselves. Life is about choices: Choosing to accept the truth of who we are, no matter what the truth may be. Choosing to love ourselves even though we may seem so different from what is considered "normal" in our society. Choosing to let go of guilt, shame, and fear. Choosing life. With that comes one simple requirement: *to be honest with yourself.* If you are not, with whom can you be honest?

Above all, life is about finding peace and being *in tune with who you really are*, so you can not only survive...but *thrive*.

Thank You

The fact that you have this book in your hands is a dream come true for me. It warms my heart that you find my story and thoughts interesting enough to spend your time reading a whole book about it, and for that I am truly grateful. Finding guidance, peace, and understanding about yourself is only as far away as the questions you ask yourself and the choices you make in each waking moment. Time is a gift; we have only a limited amount of it, and we need to enjoy it and make it the best we can, and make ourselves the best we can, if for no one else but for ourselves. It's not hard; it just takes desire, and you never know, the choices you make today could have a very positive and rewarding impact on the world!

It has been a long, often lonesome struggle at times, but I never would have made it where I am today if it were not for a great many others who have shown me the true meaning of love and compassion. My greatest hope is that I can do the same for others. To those who have thanked me for helping you on your journey, you are very welcome. All I ask is that you return the favor by staying true to yourself and by sharing your true self with the world. That's the most precious gift each of us has to give.

I would like to say some words of thanks to some very special people in my life, for without them, I would not be where I am today; if not for some of them, I would probably not *be* at all. And to all of them, for without whom this book would not have been possible.

I'd like to thank Mom and Dad for all they have given me, for sharing their love and appreciation of fine art, for their quest for greater understanding, and for giving me the chance to live. I would like to thank them for their open minds and open hearts, for they have accepted me for who I am. They made my surgery possible, which I do not think would have happened without their help. Not only did they give me life to begin with, but they have literally given me a second life as well.

I would like to thank Cindy. Although times were sometimes hard for us during the years we were a couple, Cindy's intelligence, honesty, compassionate and warm heart, and strong love have triumphed over any and all possible negative feelings, and she remains one of my closest and dearest friends. But she is far more than a friend to me, and words cannot express my love, gratitude, and thanks for her presence in my life.

I would like thank my son, Anvil, because he has never questioned who I am or been embarrassed by my presence, no matter what forms it has taken. His love never falters and his energy, sense of humor, and positive attitude are contagious! His very existence literally saved my life, at least twice. He probably has no idea what a positive effect he has had on me. I am sure he will grow up to be an incredible man, and I am infinitely proud of him.

I would also like to thank one of my best friends, Donna Rose, for her vivacious attitude about life, her sense of humor, her wit, passion for all things— especially her drive to become the woman she is and to help others in the process—but most of all, for her friendship and simply being the badass person she is. She has helped me through some of the toughest times, and in more ways than one, we are sisters in this life.

There are so many other people I would love to thank, but I don't have the time or the space to list you all. Just know that the things you have done for me have meant a lot to me. And you will always have my gratitude and love. Thank you!

References and Further Information

Recommended Reading:
Lama, Dali, and Cutler, Howard C. The Art of Happiness. Riverhead Hardcover, 1998.

Edwards, Betty. Drawing on the Right Side of the Brain. Tarcher, 1999.

Langone, Michael D. Recovery from Cults: Help for Victims of Psychological and Spiritual Abuse. W. W. Northern & Company, 1995.

Saraydarian, Haroutiun T. The Science of Becoming Oneself. TSG Publishing Foundation, 1996.

Viscott M.D., David. Emotionally Free: Letting go of the Past to Live in the Moment. McGraw-Hill, 1993.

Brown, Mildred L., and Rounsley, Chloe Ann. True Selves: Understanding Transsexualism—For Families, Friends, Coworkers, and Helping
Professionals. Jossey-Bass, 2003.

Rose, Donna. Wrapped in Blue. Living Legacy Press, 2003

Green, Jamison. Becoming a Visible Man. Vanderbilt University Press, 2004.

Finney Boylan, Jennifer. She's Not There. Broadway, 2004.

Vincent, Nora. Self-Made Man: One Woman's Journey into Manhood and Back. Viking Adult, 2006.

Garber, Marjorie. Vested Interests: Cross-Dressing & Cultural Anxiety. Routledge, 1997.

Califia, Pat. Sex Changes: The Politics of Transgenderism. Cleis Press, 2003.
Scott, Joan Wallach. Gender and the Politics of History. Columbia University Press, 1999.

Friedemann Pfäfflin, MD, et. al. International Journal of Transgenderism. The Haworth Press, 2005.

Online References:

The Website of Annah Moore. www.rightsideout.net

Harry Benjamin Standards of Care—The Standards of Care for Gender Identity Disorders (Fifth Version). The Harry Benjamin International Gender Dysphoria Association, Inc., 1998. www.tc.umn.edu/~colem001/hbigda/ hstndrd.htm.

Hormone Treatment in Transsexuals. TransGender Care. Henk Asscheman, M.D. and Louis J.G. Gooren, M.D. www.transgendercare.com/medical/hormonal/hormone-tx_assch_gooren.htm

Human Rights Campaign. Working for lesbian, gay, bisexual and transgender equal rights. www.hrc.org

National Organization for Women. NOW is dedicated to making legal, political, social and economic change in our society in order to achieve our goal, which is to eliminate sexism and end all oppression. www.now.org

Zhou, J.-N., M.A. Hofman, L.J. Gooren and D.F. Swaab. "A Sex Difference in the Human Brain and its Relation to Transsexuality." The Journal Nature. November 1995 www.nature.com/nature/journal/v378/n6552/abs/378068a0.html

STAY TRUE!

Look for Annah's follow-up to *Right Side Out* coming in 2015. She will share her journey after surgery with even more action-packed and interesting tales of adventure!

If you are interested in more work by Annah Moore, look for her new book *Lyrics of My Life*, a compilation of over 30 years of poems and song lyrics written by Ms. Moore during some of her highest highs and lowest lows. A wonderful chronicle of her life in verse.

Ms. Moore has also written a sci-fi adventure novel called *The Great, Cold Distance* which is the first of a three-part series.

Made in the USA
Monee, IL
30 August 2020

39853121R00128